The Unicorn Delusion:

How to Kill Your Inner Basic Bitch

By G.L. Lambert

For more information visit:

SolvingSingle.com

"Getting rid of a delusion makes us wiser than getting hold of a truth."

–Ludwig Borne

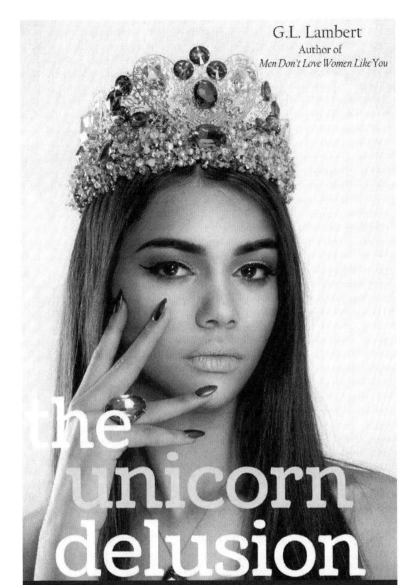

G.L. Lambert
Author of
Men Don't Love Women Like You

the
unicorn
delusion
How To Kill
Your Inner Basic B*tch

How to Kill Your Inner Basic Bitch –
The Deluxe Collection

Table of Contents

Collecting Power

*I*t's time to get back to being the powerful bad-ass woman that you know you are... when you're not in the midst of overthinking, being put to the test, dealing with anxiety, giving into petty behavior, or having a panic attack brought on by the various assholes that populate this world. Everyone needs a reset moment to catch and collect themselves. This book will serve as that hard reset for you to scan through whenever you're feeling weak, being taken advantage of, or simply burnt the fuck out. This isn't a traditional book with chapters that build towards an ending. It's a collection of several thematically similar entries that focus on the much-needed goal of extinguishing your weak traits, your negative thoughts, and your debilitating fears so you can quickly regain your place of power in your Universe.

For those unfamiliar with my work, my writing rips away the pleasantries of soft snowflake empowerment and gives it to you straight. I will curse at you, I will push your buttons, I will knock you down, all so you can pick yourself back up stronger than ever. This is a kill or be killed world. There are clear winners and clear losers. If you need kid gloves and nice language, then you already know which side you'll end up on in the 21st century. I'm not some guy trying to spoon feed you the same old regurgitated love language crap. I'm not going to show you how to text, how to submit, wait 90 days, or how to do basic shit to get men to like you. Queens don't step off their thrones to chase peasants, and don't get it confused, each one of you reading this is royal!

What makes me the expert? Why should you listen to some man tell you how to be a stronger woman? This isn't about me, it's about your truth. I'm a married man who created a website to help empower womankind and spill the tea on all the fucked up things we as men do. Guys typically don't like me, but I could care less. I've spoken around the world, and I still answer hundreds of emails a week. I have ten years of success stories and failure examples. I advise two celebrities that are household names as well as a few women who still do the opposite of everything I say. Which means I pull from the good, the bad, the lows, and the highs to help those who are open to being helped.

I gathered a few of my favorite articles from my website and expanded upon them. I also included a few bonus chapters from my actual books that were only available to a select few. The cherry on top is what I call **The Unicorn Delusion**. It's a fast and furious crash course on how to get your head out of your ass and get back on the path of what I describe as "Spartanhood." A Spartan is an Alpha Female, one who embodies confidence and aggressively puts her needs above all. Any woman can become a Spartan because the DNA of God Herself has always pumped through your veins, you were just too afraid to use it.

My job is to build Goddesses, not girls who just want boys to text back or women who just want to get married before they hit age 40. *The Unicorn Delusion* deals with the concept of the "basic bitch" a vulgar buzzword that's been overused at this point yet still aptly defines the characteristics of the anti-Spartan. **Are you basic?** I'm not talking about fashion, taste in music, or the hobbies you enjoy. This isn't a fucking Cosmo article about the *Top 10 Basic Bitch Things You Do*. This is self-analytical psychology. A basic bitch is a woman who gets pushed around, who pretends to be strong, who falls for male manipulation, who wishes she was someone else, who wears a mask in the morning and a face full of tears at night, an ego-based woman at the mercy of the world. Basic bitches are the most typical females in every city. They talk the same, they act the same, and they are painfully transparent in their want to be validated by male love. Right now, you're probably doing a mental check and confirming that you're not that basic. Cut the bullshit. I don't care which of your basic friends you compare yourself to, how much money you have, what your GPA in school averaged, or what your career title happens to be. None of that absolves you from being considered basic.

Take a hard look at your life. Have you been taken advantage of? Do you make excuses for your short-comings? Is your finger pointed at others every time you fail? Do you make defensive excuses? Are you able to walk outside and get a handsome man to take you on a nice romantic date? Are you able to walk into the next room and get your boyfriend to treat you like he did when you were considered a new vagina? Are you charismatic and engaging? Are you respected? Most importantly, *are you happy... or are you just hanging on?*

This book is for you. It has been waiting for you, and you have been waiting for it. It's short. It's to the point. It will poke a hole in the false avatar you call "self" and force you to rewrite your mind and with it your reality. Each chapter contains something different yet is glued together by the mission statement of *"You Can Do Better!"* I hope it serves to wake you from your delusion and start you on your path to Spartanhood.

The Unicorn Delusion:

How to Kill Your Inner Basic Bitch

*T*here are two groups of women I regularly speak to, those in their 20s who think their shit doesn't stink and come to me under cover of "Oh, I don't need advice, I know all of this stuff. I'm only making sure I'm not missing something." The other group are women in their 30s who are so beaten down and frustrated that they're looking for some sign that they aren't destined to settle. Unlike the 20 sometimes, the 30+ women have traded in the cocky "I KNOW I KNOW I GET IT," teeth sucking for the hopeless whimpers of, "Maybe I missed out on my soulmate and need to take what I can get..." What changes over the course of 7-10 years that humbles the fuck out of the average know it all, leaving her a shell of her former self? The reality that she **never** knew as much as she led herself to believe.

When you're young, you lack the wisdom that comes from making stupid mistakes and reflecting on them in a positive manner. You're either naïve, and in the process of making that life-altering blunder, or you're the stubborn type that puts the blame on other factors, thus never truly internalizing what to do right next time. When you grow older relationship fatigue sits in, and it cancels out the wisdom you've accumulated over the years. A decade or more of disappointment knocks a seasoned woman down, and she becomes so sick of trying to spot lies and game, that she just gives up. Hence, being 30+ and weighed down by the past to the point where you continue to use bad judgment because you're too worn out to vet or too lonely to be picky.

To be self-aware of where you are in life isn't just the key, it's the magic lamp that will lead to thriving in terms of love, money, or whatever you consider happiness. The disconnect between where you currently are in life and achieving this ultimate form of power is delusion. You're in the midst of reading a book about self-improvement—in secret. **The title of this book spoke to something deep inside, it smashed against the truth that you normally hide.** You know you're basic. You aren't happy in life because you know you can do better. There are things you should work on...there are character traits you need to improve upon...but you don't' know how. So here you are looking for the answers that will trigger real change. Reading self-help books, looking at YouTube videos, surfing the net, these are private actions where you hit pause on your delusion and seek help on everything you struggle with beneath that fake smile you put on every time you step out of the house. Right now, you're vulnerable, and I want you to stay here.

Leave your opinions outside these pages. I don't care if you agree or disagree with these points. I could care less if you have examples of someone you know or heard about who succeeded at life despite their flaws. This book is about you and only you. You're weak in ways you will never admit publicly, and I'm going to carve it out of you before it's too late. How do you make an egotistical young woman humble her know it all attitude, so she can learn these lessons without having to waste years of her life? How do you dig the bitterness out of an older woman and prove to her that it's not too late? You kill the delusion.

The Circle of Basic

The 34-year-old that wasted five years of her 20s with a fuck boy, then rushed into a bad rebound relationship instead of healing, is just the older version of the 24-year-old that's currently writing me about how to let go of her on again off again boyfriend. Here's how the circle goes: That 24-year-old won't take my advice, she'll fake like she's a Spartan for a week, then get lonely or fall for some text paragraph from her dick head boyfriend. They'll get back together, and it'll be perfect for about a month, then it'll devolve back to the hellhole relationship it was always meant to be. *Fast forward a few years later...* she will contact me again, saying that she wished she would have listened as the boyfriend is now gone, off posting new women on his social media or engaged to some chick who's half as cute. **She'll question how a man that loved her quickly moved on**. Meanwhile she feels like a loser for putting all that effort in for nothing. I will once again give her the best advice I can, which she will only take seriously until the next guy pops up calling her pretty and showering her with attention.

The moment *New Dick* comes on the scene, she'll revert to the Basic Bitch she's so accustomed to being. New Dick will waste another year, maybe two stringing her along, and then Miss Sassy Sexy 24 will look in the mirror and see Miss Beaten Down 34 and realize that she's spent the past ten years dealing with men that never really wanted her. What hurts is that the men she was stuck on were never smarter than her nor did they pull the wool over her eyes with genius scams. Miss Beaten Down saw the red flags, but she kept playing along because—say it with me—*Bored women with nothing to do entertain clowns*! It's her bad and she knows it, and now she's motivated to change, for real this time.

Hold up! At this point her face isn't as fresh, her hips are a little larger, her social circle has shrunk, and her confidence to go out and date properly is shot because she's spent a decade having her self-esteem lowered. While she's motivated, she's no longer that vibrant young thing with options. She gets in her head about what can go wrong. She freezes up when she's in public and face to face with a handsome man. She says dumb shit like, "I'm happy single," only because she doesn't know how to start over. She pays for dating sites and takes chances on past guys who reach out on Facebook because she's desperate. That's how that 24-year-old transforms into that desperate and burnt 34-year-old who goes to sleep thinking, "why didn't I listen? Why didn't I pick better? Why didn't I see through the game?"

You most likely fall into one of those categories: <u>Young arrogant and ignorant or aging annoyed and insecure.</u> I want to uplift you right here and right now, so you can begin to turn that corner and follow the path of love, money, or any form of abundance you desire to a positive result. I've written books that go in detail on how to attain, but what good are they if you can't go out and do it? To help you use any of my full books, specifically <u>Men Don't Love Women Like You</u> to the best of your ability, I must burst your basic bubble, destroy the false self, and rebuild a Spartan Queen on the foundation of truth. That sounds abstract or over your head now, but by the end, you will not only get it, you will see that's the only way to win this game.

A unicorn, that's what all women believe they are. Something different and special, a creature that a man should be honored to have because of these extraordinary things you and only you do—bitch, please. It's time to kill the delusion that you're currently doing anything extraodinary, and accept that if your results have been trash, it's because your attitude, personality, or conversation, are all mediocre! Go ahead and get defensive, say it's the men who don't know how to treat a unicorn. Blame it on your age group or your city. I'll wait... When you're done pointing fingers, look at the full board. Real unicorns win every day!

I had three women who used to email me for advice get married last year. I know four more personal friends that got married last year. All 7 of them had to kill their inner basic bitch before they could graduate to that level. Women are out here winning, and men are out here recognizing a good thing. For each excuse you pull out of your ass, I can point you to someone who overcame. Look to your own life. Your friend, your work associate, your cousin, someone you know is happy and in love, right? How are they doing better in life than you Ms. Unicorn? Because you're too close to the subject be honest about how average you are. Like a mother with an ugly kid, you are biased! It's time to look in the mirror and get to the truth of you, rip out that ego, and evolve! Below are traits that Basicas (my pet term for Basic Bitches) hold up as proof that they aren't typical. Let's go one by one and destroy these false concepts.

My Looks Are Special

False Wisdom of Your 20's: You're young and vibrant, and you're still in an active social scene where no matter if you're at the high end of the so-called *Dime Spectrum* or the low end of *She's A'ight*, you constantly get hit on. Even if you're getting approached by guys that aren't your type, the results are still the same—*These boys are on me!* That's the kind of confidence most women would kill for. To know that your sexiness is not just in your head, that you can actually turn heads and get approached, swells you with pride. The wisdom of the male agenda hasn't settled in at this point, and you buy into the hype that if a guy goes after you, he <u>must</u> like you. *You're girlfriend pretty, why else would he break his neck to get your number... You're wifey material, why else would he be trying to take you out on a date... You must look better than all the other girls he talks to or else he would keep wanting to see you...*

Now you reach the next level: Overconfidence. Why should you vet him or test his intentions when a man's acting like your groupie? At this point, he likes you more than you like him, which means that on top of the initial sexual attraction and lusty energy bubbling inside, you also have the rush of power and control that comes from having a man hanging from your clit. You foolishly believe that he will act right to gain exclusive rights and keep those exclusive rights because his actions all point to him being your number one fan. Logically you point to his initial consistently as proof that he's not going to play you. Emotionally you're invincible because you believe in the myth that a man will come correct for a pretty girl. Reality will show you that these kinds of men are usually sneaky and must be vetted, but at this point in your life story, overconfidence blinds you to this fact.

False Wisdom of Your 30's: The older you get, the more your *Dating Pools* changes (for a step by step breakdown of each Dating Pool read *She Ain't It*). Meaning that whereas you were in school and meeting tons of boys or clubbing in your 20s meeting cute guys every time you went out, at this point in life you settle into a routine. Your crew doesn't really turn up, they do brunch. Your weekends are for running errands, not mingling. You don't bump into new men often, unless it's a newbie at work, the gym, or one that moves into your neighborhood. Unlike girls in their 20s, you aren't getting hit on as much either. Predictably this lowers your confidence. You post a new profile picture on Facebook, and you get likes, big deal, everyone gets that shit. You go to the market and get a few stares, but no one approaches. You get dolled up for those few occasions where you go out, and maybe you get attention, but it's not overwhelming like it was back in the day. The worst feeling is when a guy does break his neck to talk to you he's either an older man whose thirsty for something young(er) or some busted guy that makes your pussy dry up. "Damn, am I ugly? Why am I attracting these Meth Addict looking guys!?"

This is the foundation that becomes your new normal, limited options and a feeling of hopelessness. Enter a decent looking man that chases after you, flatters you, and looks at you like you're a feast. What does that do to you mentally? It stuns the wisdom you built up, and you revert to that naïve woman from seven years ago that felt overconfident. You know that men are fairer weather than Laker fans, but you entertain it because to be looked at as if you're the sexiest bitch in the room and be told how perfect you are, flaws and all, feels damn good. All that time alone or dealing with bums makes attention from guys you would actually date, feel so fucking sweet. Once again, all the testing of this man goes out the window as you feel that you're the prize.

Then Reality Hits: The novelty of a pretty face fades. As men, we impulsively chase after girls for dozens of reasons, the top being her looks, but once we get you, spend time with you, see you in different outfits, hairstyles, with makeup and without, **your beauty becomes ordinary.** Think about your bedroom and the pictures on the wall, the first week after you hang them up, it's impressive, then a few months later they become just a part of the paint. Someone will come over and compliment a picture, and you'll be like, "oh, yeah...thanks." You have to be reminded of the beauty because we take things we see all the time for granted. The same applies to women. Your eyes don't stop being pretty, your ass doesn't deflate, your face isn't less appealing, but to the man that was only impressed by those traits and nothing else, it's no longer a big deal. Hence, a few months in and he's gone from being your groupie to not having time to see you, to wanting to spend time with his friends more often, or even chasing other women who may not be as attractive as you. Never buy into the hustle that you're so pretty that a man will want you forever. Most of us just want to borrow, not buy!

Look at Ms. Young & Fit whose body shuts down Instagram on the daily. Let me test drive that tight young body for a few weeks and get my nut off. After I have my fun I'll move on to the next because I didn't actually like you or anything you were talking about, I was merely lusting after you like every other dude with a dick and free time.

Look at Ms. Mature & Thick who knows how to fill out a dress and who I don't have to worry about taking care of because she has her career on track. Let me get a fetish nut off for a few months, then fall back because I didn't actually want her old damaged ass beyond the physical just like every other guy that shares the same body type fetish.

Men are predators, first, romantics second! No matter what category you fall into or what physical trait on you leads to attention, never let male attention drop you onto a false throne of power. He thinks you're cute, so what? He's up your ass and trying to see you, so what? He's giving you compliment after compliment, so what? What does this man want from you for real? Is it sex? Is it a trophy? Is it a girlfriend? Is it a wife? Don't jump to the answer you want, take your time and get the real answer he shows over time. The more a man likes a woman, the more typical females like him back because most are attention whores, literally selling out just because someone's stroking that ego. Real relationships aren't based on shallow attractions, they're constructed slowly based on compatibility. "I like him because he likes me a lot," is the dumbest concept ever when you uncover the truth that being a fan of your physical is not the same as being in love with your personality.

The delusion that you're too pretty to get played will stick with you even when you get played because you will refuse to believe it was just lust or just a sexual mission. For instance, I knew a young woman who swore to me that the reason a guy kept her as a *friend with benefit* rather than commit to her was because he was so busy with work. "He's not going to do better" were her exact words and she just knew that eventually he would get a break in work and they would be together. Wrong. He ended up making some other girl his woman. **Same man, same work schedule, but suddenly he had all this free time to court and commit to another woman.** Her hubris was tied to her looks, even after she got served humble pie, she tracked down the girl's Facebook profile, befriended her from a false account, and emailed me several pictures asking, "No way she's prettier than me, right?" This little Basica missed the entire point of what makes a man choose wifey over pussy—character. Which transitions us perfectly into the next section...

My Personality Is Special

False Wisdom of Your 20s: You're young, hip, and silly which translate to your friends enjoying your company and strangers positively reacting to you because your energy is lit. No matter if you're the shy one in the group or the leader, your sense of humor is appreciated, your advice is sought out, and being of the millennial generation, you stay woke. This forms an inflated sense of coolness and even intelligence to the point where you stop being self-aware. Your girlfriends talk behind your back, but they won't bring up the contradictorily shit you do or the moods that bother them to your face. Your friends are like your sisters, so it's accepted with a silent shrug. However, boys that want to fuck you, are they really impressed with you or are they playing along?

Now, this is where it really gets messy. Guys will text you all day about a bunch of nothing as a prelude to asking when they will get to see you next. The conversation isn't about you, it's about your schedule, and you already know why. Yet, you still smile when you get that text and rush to pick out something to wear, even if it is just a house date. If you're not texting about seeing each other, it's all about flirting. Men flirt to induce sexting or at the least get you comfortable enough to tease him with the idea that you may be a bad girl when you do meet face to face. At this point you're not asking if this man likes you or the kind of opinion he's forming about your character, you assume that he thinks you're bomb as fuck because he keeps sending "good morning beautiful," texts before work and "wyd" texts in the afternoon. None of these text conversations are showing a man that you're any different from the next woman, nor is this man texting topics to delve into your personality. **It's all light conversation to prime you for his dick.** He could care less about the last book you read or who gave you a nasty look in the break room at work, through flirt texting and asking to see you he gets what he came for—pussy.

On your dates, some of you may argue that you spend all night talking about real life and you connect on a deep level: *This world is so unfair, the prison system is a scam, the earth is warming out of control, you want to start a business, he wants to start one too, wouldn't traveling be nice, you both miss the old Kanye...* then you finish off with half-ass rundowns of your past relationships that make you both look like the victims. **No one cares, and none of that shit is impressive.** "GL, our chemistry is crazy!" is a phrase I hear at least once a month from women telling me about some new prospect. You're of the same generation, and of the same liberal ideology, of course, you're going to have chemistry when you both believe the same shit, and both find each other attractive physically. It's not your personality, it's parody. At this stage, the things I've written about in terms of vetting or *Dating Like a Spartan* aren't in your head reminding you to open up the topics and dig into the past. You don't need advice, nor do you want to think about agenda. You're grinning, turned on, and your ego is moist from him agreeing with your points and "wowing" at how smart you are. You aren't going to test him after this, he gets you and you get him on the shallowest level, and that's good enough.

False Wisdom of Your 30s: Older, much more well read, and able to hold a conversation about many topics, as an older woman you satisfy a man's mind and this trait will make you the wifey type in the long run. Being well cultured is always a positive, but there's a difference between knowing things and being a know it all. Men nod along and hit you with, "you're right," a lot because guys in your older Dating Pool also come with a lifetime of knowledge and opinions. The biggest lesson we men learn is, "let her talk..." at first anyway. This translate to a man who is just getting to know you letting you broadcast your opinion unchecked. Politics, entertainment, and the most talked about topic—men and women, are greeted with little blowback because your date isn't trying to say the wrong thing to turn you off. Unlike a young man who will raise his voice and argue about how men and women should both split bills in a household or that 9/11 was an inside job, an older man isn't interested in hypothetical debates that damage his image. Older men are astute and patient.

The wisdom of age lets an older woman continue to live out her fantasy that she's the most interesting creature in the world and right about everything she opens her mouth to speak on. Thus the conversation topics stay llimited and safe, which means the man doesn't have to worry about saying the wrong thing to ruin his shot at your pussy. Your daily opinions on current events, your excuses on how your past setbacks weren't your fault, your critique of other women as bum bitches, and of course your disdain for *ain't shit* men and what they need to do to be better, is what you end up talking about. All he says is that he works a good job and his ex wasn't a good fit, and you buy it. There will be no real vetting of his story or background because you're excited to talk about all the shit you know, and like any smart man looking to snatch the cookies, he lets you go on and on.

Then Reality Hits: Most of you don't talk about shit and the other half dumb down your conversation to fit in. So, how is your personality being projected? Are you truly seen as "cool" or are you annoying? Sure you're book smart, but are you engaging? These are the things self-aware must know to avoid being delusional about their personality. I once advised this lady in her mid-20s who was dating an NBA player. Her first question to me was about topics she could bring up to make her seem cool to him. Should she talk about basketball, or does every groupie ho do that? Should she ask about his family and his childhood, or is that being too personal? Should she talk about video games, Marvel movies, and other generic guy shit? I asked why she hadn't developed the skills to relate to the opposite sex in her 25 years on the planet. Her response, "I know how to talk to boys, but this is different." I later found out she didn't know how to talk to boys at all. She was the kind of woman that didn't talk about shit, who would text nudes and selfies then utilize flirty language to entice men to want to like her. Like many of you, she was awkward unless she was getting smart and sassy, or being nasty. She was ill prepared to spark a good conversation with what she now saw as her meal ticket and realized that her personality wasn't as bomb as she was led to believe. Just another **Zombie with a Pussy**.

On the issue of dumbing down, that's almost as common. For instance, there was a girl who's Facebook page was all political and spiritual. Dump Trump, Vision Boards, links to all kinds of social injustice protests and donation sites. I knew her in real life, and the moment she got around this potential boyfriend a mutual friend tried to hook her up with, she reverted to a little girl. She didn't talk about politics, spirituality, or any of that shit from her online persona. She just giggled, nodded along, and made the occasional sassy joke. She and the guy ended up in a situationship for a few months, and that's when she asked me how she to take it to the next level. After hearing how their relationship operated it was clear she was being played. Even more ironic is that the woman that couldn't shut up on social media was voiceless in this so-called relationship.

They had nothing in common, but sexual attraction. They didn't talk about anything deeper than movies and places to order food. Yet she still wanted him because she was lonely, and he was more attractive than the guys she normally talked to. Her want to be some incompatible man's chick was more than her need to express her viewpoints with a partner, which made her personality half of what I knew it to be. The moment she tried to stand her ground he fell back and got a new chick, and she was back to posting ten times a day about the injustice of the world. Think about that. So many women run around talking about "stay woke" yet have a man in their phone playing them. Who's really sleep?

Let's switch to older women who believe they're so smart and cultured and how they get caught up by the wolves. The moment a know-it-all makes it out of that honeymoon phase where a man nods along, those seemingly perfect guys reveal their true colors. He thinks your opinions are dumb, and can now check you with, "What are you talking about, that's not at all how it happened." He can play with his phone while you motor on about how some girl at work shouldn't get married to her cheating fiancé because now he doesn't have to front like you're some advice guru. **You're just another chick with a hot take on what others should be doing with their life.** Once he starts talking back, ignoring you, or making light of the things you think you know, the fighting starts. You're older and stubborn, and so is he. What I witness is that the men win out because the older the woman, the more likely she is to fall in line, so this asshole won't leave her single again. An older man understands the power of imbedding himself in a woman's life. A month or two of him being a perfect gentleman that worships the ground you walk on feels like a lifetime. Are you going to walk away three months in once he starts to become less consistent or tell you that your work drama is stupid? Not if you're the typical female. You put up with his bullshit, you remember how good he was during that first month, you allow him to slide and slide until it's too late.

Think about the average relationship between two people that aren't compatible: *You talk to vent or complain. You talk to arrange when to see each other. You talk to gossip.* In between those talks you argue with each other about something the other did. What happened to the talks about your business plans or goals? What happened to the vacation ideas or shared taste in music? Why is this man now spending time with other guys more than you? Because his boys actually have shit to talk about that excites him. Why is this man now having an emotional affair with another woman? Because even with her clothes on she gets him more than you do. You have to get this idea that flirting and venting is talking and that by having opinionated conversations you're showing how bomb your personality is. Men are impressed by women who don't talk the same shit as other women. Men are impressed by women that ask questions and follow-ups to prove that they aren't suckers for sex baiting. How can anyone respect your mind if you aren't giving them anything more than basic bitch conversation? When you do all the talking and refuse to dig into a man's life, you prove how average you are.

My Vagina Is Special

False Wisdom of Your 20s: Men moan and cum fast when inside a tight vagina. Men grunt, "*I love you... tell me it's mine... you better never give Daddy's pussy away... I want this forever...*" like your tight vagina is Wonder Woman's lasso of truth. Men roll over to get another round in because you're that good. Men call the next day to get another round in because you're that insatiable. Men will even call a year later to get another round in... all because they realize no other woman can do what you do. When you're young and sexually active, the statistics will read: ***Made every man I slept with cum fast and hard.***

You're ignoring the fact that other women can claim the <u>same</u> thing. Instead, you focus on what men say. "I've had some trash pussy... girls today don't know how to fuck... you're the best I've ever had." It's lip service! You want to believe that out of all the girls in the world you're one of the talented few that get men sprung. If this were the Scientific Method, a professor would tell you to go out and talk to other women and compare notes to see what percent are told they have trash pussy or if they too are told they're the best ever. But this isn't science, it's ego, and you want to believe you're special, so that's what you believe.

The man you're sleeping with, be it your boyfriend or just a friend with benefits, is tied to you because he can never leave the best pussy he ever had. Men don't ever lie or exaggerate, so his praise MUST be true, right? Ha! Other women are getting their bills paid, trips to the YSL store, condos bought, locked down in real relationships, and you barely get a birthday gift—*but your pussy is bomb, right?* Your exes have all moved on, even those that call you for a rematch, don't really want you on a girlfriend level—*but your pussy is bomb, right?* In your 20s you don't let facts fuck up a good myth. You make men cum, you make men keep calling, you even have guys with girlfriends trying to hit again, that means something, and you refuse to believe that millions of other women can claim the same thing—you're unique.

False Wisdom of Your 30s: Wisdom is Enlightenment, and any woman that's survived her 20s now realizes the hard truth—**men will put their dicks in just about anything**

when horny. Plot Twist: Men are always horny. As an older woman, you're no longer fueled by the arrogance that your vagina is the only one that yanks. You've had multiple men collapse on top of you with "I love you," or "I want to have a baby," and now realize that men like to talk when in the moment, but rarely mean any of those things once the lust dissipates. <u>There's no such thing as a magical vagina, they're all created equally.</u> Some get wetter depending on the man, which can make the experience better. Some are tighter, which can make the experience better. At this age, you aren't ignorant to what truly makes sex stand out—the build-up and mental warfare.

Sex is a mental game, so while the 20-year-old can just lay there and say, "Oh my god," and make a man cum, it's not going to be as memorable as the girl that can do some real freak shit he'll go to sleep dreaming about. Talk to a younger woman, sex toys, licking anything besides a dick, bondage, etc... those things aren't often on their list of skills. It's more about going over his place, doing a little oral, and having sex in one of the three positions. That generic shit is all they need because young women think Odin bestowed them with an enchanted pussy. A woman that's 30+ is getting her Vivica Fox on. Meaning she's licking ass, she's introducing dildos and vibrators, she's role-playing as a school teacher, and she's making a sexual encounter more than a hole a man thrust into until climax. **While a younger girl with a fresh face and tight body may be visually appealing, they can't compete mentally with the experience of an older woman in her sexual prime who isn't too shy to be nasty.** This is the secret superpower older women are waiting to unleash because that's the true definition of "bomb pussy" that will make her a must have. The wisdom is there, but once again the ego blinds. Older women are quicker to have sex because true blue adults don't have time to play those waiting games. The problem isn't having sex too fast at this age, it's confusing his love of your sex skills with his love of your personality.

Then Reality Hits: Sex is honey, not glue! Where are all the men that have had sex with you right now? What has their praise gotten you in your life? Most of them didn't even make you cum, yet you're holding on to their hollow words or their premature ejaculation as proof that you're Rey from *Star Wars*. Men are in love with the pursuit of sex—that's why they trick to get it. Men have a fetish for being filthy when their dicks are hard—that's why they exaggerate during the process and say things they don't mean. Men have an insatiable greed for something new—that's why no matter how good your pussy is, he will most likely trade you in for the next girl.

It's not about Kegel exercises, whip cream, or going ass to mouth until his toes curls. **The glue you're looking for doesn't require you to take off your clothes at all.** What makes a man stay after the lust leaves? What makes a man pass up new pussy? What makes a man still love you even when you both are too busy to have sex most nights? Your personality. Those conversations. Those shared life experiences. That mutual understanding. The partnership that dictates that you push each other to be better. None of that has shit to do with the ability to put your legs behind your head or ride a dick with no hands. Good sex is amazing, we all love it. But as I wrote in _Solving Single_, all pussy expires. To that point, all Dick expires. Just like beauty becomes ordinary, there will come a time where the new excitement of those first months or even the first year, gives way to "nice sessions." The adrenaline that pumps when you're about to lay with someone new makes your heart beat out of your chest. You can still have amazing sex for years upon years, but let's not pretend your heart still races like it did during that first week. Stop putting stock into sex as if it's going to make you irreplaceable because those basic women who don't have anything deeper than a vagina to bring into a relationship will always be replaced by a newer version.

Read Your Self

You aren't girlfriend pretty enough for him to want to be with you. You aren't smart enough for him to take you seriously. You aren't adventurous enough to keep his attention. You aren't any of the things you pop off about to your friends or online — you're a fraud. You lie to keep from crying. You argue with everyone because you're miserable inside. You talk bitterly about men and women alike because you hate that other people are happy. You keep telling yourself you're better than average, but we both know you're not proud of how your life is going or where you currently are. Go to church, read a self-help book, let your mother give you a pep talk about "in due time," and it bandages you up for a week, then you're depressed again because it's all bullshit. That's what they call A READ, and some, if not all, of those things currently apply to you. Stop letting others read you and trigger your insecurities and start reading yourself. Go step by step, flaw by flaw, trauma by trauma, lie by lie, and unravel the image you want to portray from the woman you are currently.

Step 1 – Isolate: Stop dating. Stop collecting numbers. Stop entertaining the guys that inbox you. Stop picking up the phone for anything that's romantic in nature. "But I'm so bored and lonely," fuck your loneliness! Can an alcoholic get sober in a bar? No! Which means you can't get healthy and reset your basic ways if you're in the process of trying to find love using the same old tools. **You must walk away, then come back to the game.** You can't level up in the middle of the game because there's too much of the old you inside, and the skills to do things properly haven't been tested yet. You need time alone.

Step 2 – Learn: When women come to me for advice, I first ask them which of my books have they read. If they haven't read any, or only read the website, then I'm going to waste too much time giving a summary of something that's too deep to summarize. Read *Men Don't Love Women Like You* or listen to the audio version. Let it wash over you. Sit with it, understand it, see how it fits into your life in terms of hitting reset on your past and creating a new Spartan Avatar. Read. Highlight. Read again!

Step 3 – Affirm: Live like a Spartan for a day. Build your universe. Do tests of manifesting and thought control. Know the truth for yourself. See the results for yourself. Know what it means to live in power for once, not ego. Then you do it again the next day. **Give yourself at least 4 weeks of living in power**. It's like working a muscle, a trainer can show you how to lift weights, put it's on you to do it right each time and see the gains in your strength. Be patient, work at it each day, and grow stronger.

Step 4 – Pillage: This is when you get back into the game. Not to date your exes or to try to go back to something broken, but to exercise this new Spartan power on new men. Use what you have to now get what you want, be it love, money, a promotion, it doesn't matter. It's your world at this point, conquer it!

Step 5 – Look Back: The woman you were was basic, she was easy to trigger, she was using crutch after crutch to prove that she belonged and deserved. The new you will be able to meditate on that past life and laugh at how ignorant you were to the ways of your True Self. Read this book again, read the old articles I wrote, and see all the hidden things you missed because you weren't truly woke yet. Know that you are a creator, not a slave. At this point, when it all makes sense, when you aren't tied to excuses, when you can easily see through the jesters of the world, when you have nothing to that scares or worries you, then and only then, you will have become a true Unicorn.

I, Unicorn

What makes you special has nothing to do with what you can do for a man, how much better you are than rival women, nor does it rely on your looks. Self-Confidence isn't the same as Self-Delusion. When you're delusional about how great you are, that's a foundation built upon false crutches. When you're confident in yourself, that's a foundation built upon security and self-awareness. The truth is that there will always be women that have prettier faces, better bodies or are simply what a man is looking for due to his own personal tastes. The truth is there will always be women that are into subjects you can't have a conversation about or who have traveled and lived lives that you haven't. The truth is that the man you're having the best sex of your life with will move on and tell the next girl the same things he told you, and this time around he may even marry her. What happens when your delusion runs out of track? Depression hits as you tumble into the abyss of, *"why aren't I ever good enough."* I talk to women all the time, and no matter the age, their inability to get what they want in life all boils down to a lack of self-confidence. To find your truth isn't about giving up and admitting you're not as good as other people. It's about getting out of the struggle to be better than other people because other people aren't real.

If I were to ask you to go write a list of five things you do that no other woman does, you would either lie or fail. The goal isn't to be different from other women, the goal is to be the only fucking woman in your universe and make all comparisons, bragging, and thirst to compete meaningless. A Unicorn wouldn't keep trotting over to see what the horses in the stable are doing, it lives in a world of its own where there's no need to envy or outdo. That's where you must go mentally—the internal world of supreme confidence! You don't have to tell anyone you're different from the next, your existence speaks for itself. When you go on dates, you approach it differently. When you text back, you respond differently. When you enter a relationship, you partner with your man differently. When you push him down to ride that dick, you grind differently. You know it's different because your results will be unlike anything you've experienced before.

It's on you to get there by killing those basic bitch ways. The false beliefs I laid out above are real masks that too many women wear. Your job. Your Looks. Your Coolness. Those things you hoist as impressive are typical. You must unlearn your ego. All the bullshit you think makes you hot shit, all the crutches you use to stunt on other people, they haven't worked! You still get played with, you still attract bums that can't do anything for you, you're still giving away pussy and time to guys that prove to be fraudulent, and that's a result of bad choices based on a weak delusional sense of who you are. Kill ego and envy falls with it. Kill ego and pressure falls with it. Kill ego and all the secrets of the Universe will be revealed, I'm talking literally!

You're a Spartan Queen, a goddess in the flesh, you have a fire inside of you that can't be extinguished, and it's time to turn up the heat and be more than the basic woman that wants to fit in and be liked. Different is being brave enough to remove the mask you used to call "self." Different is being unapologetically true to that self while the rest of the world tap dances for approval. Different is ingrained in your DNA, you just need a reminder...

Understanding the Opposite Sex

How to Spot A Fraudulent Man

*W*hen I tell you to "go inside" and kill delusion or to be honest about your flaws do you truly understand what that means? Spiritual concepts and theories about being a *Goddess in the flesh*, sound good, but how can you imprint that into your brain so that you feel that power as opposed to that nagging feeling that it's all bullshit and you'll never win? Think about religion for a moment. Those deep-rooted beliefs in a higher power didn't happen overnight it was generational brainwashing. Pagans, Jews, Christians, Muslims, onward to the current New Age folks. At each step, someone had to hammer that belief into the next generation with some sort of proof that made it more than just faith. I don't want you to take anything written in this book on faith. **I want to prove it to you**. You <u>are</u> a Goddess. You are the master of your own universe. Your thoughts create your reality. You can have whatever you want. Nevertheless, let's start with baby steps. You can't do the heavy lifting of manifesting real change unless you know yourself. Since this book is about separating your character from the pack of typical and delusional basic bitches, let's start by proving that the mindset that you walk around with is the only thing holding you back from becoming the Neo of your Matrix.

9 out of 10 women reading this are dishonest. I'm not talking about telling lies or stealing, I mean dishonest in terms that they can't even admit to themselves who they are and what they want for fear of being looked down upon. I once asked a girl who was going through drama with her boyfriend what she wanted from him, a relationship or a friendship? She responded that she didn't have time for any of that because she was going to school and had to figure out her next move after graduation. I didn't ask her shit about school or work goals, I asked her straight up what she

wanted from the guy she was spending her nights stressing over. Her pride wouldn't allow her to be honest enough to say, "*Yes, I like him, and I would like to be with him, but I'm afraid he doesn't want the same– help.*" She gave me a bullshit answer that wouldn't make her seem weak, soft, or thirsty. The more insecure the woman, the harder she tries to hide her insecurity behind attitude and excuses. No one can help you if you're too prideful to admit what you want and that you're afraid you won't get it.

To safeguard their feelings, some women drape a cloak of "I'm good" over themselves and pretend that they don't care about anything. *I don't want him to spend time with me, I'm busy anyway*—Stop Lying. *I don't want him to put me first, I'm not trying to be his girl anyway*—Stop Lying. *I don't want other people to like me, I'm a lone wolf*—Stop Lying. *I don't want him to ask me to be official, I'm not looking for anything serious anyway*—Stop Lying!

To even bring up, "I'm not even worried about him," is an admission of being worried about him, or else you wouldn't have brought him up! I'm going to let you in on a secret, men don't believe you, that's why they call your bluff, toy with your emotions, and act as if they don't care—your apathy is transparent. Sad, lonely, and angry women make bad relationship choices because their actions don't match the words coming out of their mouths. Players eat passive and defensive women for breakfast because their buttons are out in the open and easy to push. So why do you lie to yourself?

When a person thinks they will fail at something or be rejected, they become passive and act if they weren't trying in the first place. This way if they don't get the results they really want, it won't seem like they failed. **Read that again and understand it because you are guilty of doing it.** *Single and happy, focusing on me, raising my child, waiting on Jesus to return, blah blah blah.* That's all bullshit. You can front like you're not on the racetrack, but we know that you're still secretly in the race hoping to get chose! How do I know that's true? When a seemingly perfect man slides you his number, you don't delete it, you get excited, all of those excuses go out the window, and all you can think of is, "*Please God let this one be The One.*" YOU. ARE. NOT. HONEST. The only thing that will save you from being played is to be honest about your shortcomings. Your character is flawed and boggled down with fear and dishonesty. If you are to become that "Goddess in the flesh" instead of a typical delusional bird, this is the first thing you must come to grips with. The fact that you are full of shit.

If you aren't real enough to say, "The reason I want to call this man and yell at him for not calling me all week, isn't because I love him, but because I have a weakness for attention and affection because my father never gave me that," then you will confuse love of attention with love of that person. Those women that can self-diagnose themselves don't have anxiety, they don't cry, they don't snap, they don't blow up a dude's phone, and they don't ask every one of their friends their opinion on "What do you think he means by this text."

To be honest about your flaws is to be free of male manipulation because men can't pull your strings if you've already cut those motherfuckers. This chapter will advance your power. Now that you understand that you must be honest about your own flaws to become a true Unicorn, the second step is being honest about the opposite sex and their agenda. This is your world, your amusement park, your video game. However, it isn't populated with nice, vanilla people who are nice and honest. The men that populate your world are there to test you. They are fool's gold, actual gold, and plain old lead. The hard work isn't finding men to date, each one of you can attract dates. The hard work is figuring out who is worth your time and who is simply trying to waste it. Let's go over the mind of a few types of men you will meet in your journey. I suggest you frequently highlight as this chapter will become a life saver...

The Mindset of Men with Options

Women claim they don't compete with other women, but Instagram, Twitter, Facebook, the breakrooms at work, and the line to get into the clubs, all prove that's a lie. My entire life I assumed women were being honest when they said, "I'm not worried about the next bitch." Then I started my website, began to get hundreds of emails a week, and saw actual proof that the average woman does nothing but worry about the next chick. Men aren't rare, they aren't special, but we as males know that if we promote that we are one of "the good ones" you will treat us like our dicks are dipped in Vibranium from Wakanda!

Men have options, the same as women, but men exercise their options more blatantly. For instance, if you were to meet a professional man making good money and had good looks to match, you should date him under the same rules you date any man, value, respect, and communication, right? Wrong. Men know that women today think, "If I like him, she likes him, and she may get him unless I give in and let him take me on house date." **The moment you let "He has other women after him" dictate how you treat a man, then you lose!** When you're in a relationship, and you allow "He has other women trying to take him" lower the bar on how he should treat you, you're going to always get shortchanged. Men, even the dumb ones, are smart enough to use other women as leverage because it works. This fool is going to use the fact that he can get easier pussy tomorrow to force you into giving him easy pussy today. Think about that... You're a slave to the fear that some other woman can steal the guy you're texting, dating, or in a relationship with, so you let these guys get away with more than a woman who is truly a Unicorn would allow.

If you were truly honest, you could admit, "I really like him, and I don't think I can do better, so I'm going to submit." Then I could smack you in the back of your head and remind you that you could do better if you aimed high and Spartan'd up.

However, if you bury that insecurity and fear, you won't understand why you are competing for this man, and you'll continue to reactively submit because you can't stop the want for him. It's not enough to understand why a man is treating you a certain way, it's much more important to understand why you are allowing him to get away with it.

Unlike Dua Lipa, you don't need 3 rules, you only need one: **Don't treat a man as if he's special**. No matter if he's the cutest guy at your school, the owner of the company you work for, your twitter crush, a celebrity, or athlete. You have to be willing to risk him walking away then to bend the knee and give him special treatment. We as males, don't pay attention to much, but we notice what women let us get away with not texting, not going on real dates, and who falls for "I'm so busy with work," excuses. The more a woman allows us to pick her up and put her down, the more power we have over her. A woman that has other options won't put up with what women with no options will. A woman that sees us as a catch can play hard to get, but by testing her through a series of games, we can see if she's thirsty or not. This is the mindset we men walk around with, and why we can pretend not to care. It's all a game or better yet, a "bitch-check" to break women down. A Unicorn can't be bitch checked because she doesn't mind putting her foot down and setting ground rules. "I don't want to scare him away by being too demanding," is the best kind of female mentality when you're looking to exploit pussy. Now that you know this be the woman that vets a man, risks a man, and follows the rule listed above. Watch how your dating life changes...

The Mindset of Emotionally Abusive Men

Women hate to be told about themselves, but they love to be told about themselves. It's mental BDSM, that would make Christian Grey envious. On the surface, most women pretend to be strong, but they get off on a man that can call bullshit and push their insecure little buttons. I promote the concept of "read yourself" but so many women can't, thus they become slaves to men who can sniff out their damage.

I remember one girl telling me how her Situationship guy (*aka Friend with Benefits/Talking but not exclusive*) shitted on her about not having a car, as if not driving meant that she was a loser. She ranted about it to me, then followed up a week later with, "So I fucked him, and afterwards he started downing me about being my age and still living with my parents." Wait Wait Wait! **A man calls you a bum bitch, and to prove him wrong you go and ride him like the car you can't afford?** This shit would be funny if it weren't so tragic. There are women who are so insecure and self-loathing that they react to verbal abuse like a finger rubbing against their clit. *Yes, tell me how I'm pathetic and work a low paying job, I'm about to cum so hard!*

A woman with confidence and self-esteem would delete that guy's number the moment he came at her neck with non-constructive criticism, but weak bitches long to prove themselves worthy. I repeat for the millionth time, have to know your flaws instead of pretending that it doesn't bother you because an intelligent man will take you on one date and break your weak ass down in all the areas where you pretend to be strong at in order to get you to fall in line. You have a big nose, so he's going to show you a picture of the last chick he was with that's two times as pretty as you. You don't have much money, he's going to brag about his career and guilt you about not being on his level. You ran your mouth about how your last boyfriend cheated on you, he's going to wait until you act up and say, "I see why guys cheat on you." You have a child, he's going to remind you that nobody wants a used bitch with an already made family. By the time he's done defecating on your soul, you'll be begging him to fuck you and give you his approval. It's game! He's playing Lee Harvey Oswald with your self-esteem, and you're a sitting duck because you aren't strong enough to love yourself!

Yes, you are flawed, yes you have made mistakes, but you don't need to be admonished by any man! Stop dressing in cardboard and thinking that shit is armor. Be honest about your shortcomings and fix them instead of waiting for a man to come and exploit them. The male mind is similar to a computer hacker, the job is to push and push until you find a hole to slip through. An emotionally abusive man listens to your trauma, then he turns it back on you in a way that strips away all that "fake strong" woman empowerment shit you talk about. Each one of you has an issue that you don't like to talk about. This could be your parents, a sexual assault, your looks, or past rejection. When I say fix them, I understand it's not that easy, but you start by pinpointing it first. This is where the lessons of *Men Don't Love Women Like You* come in, as the first half of that book is all about resetting past trauma. Nevertheless, if you're currently dating, watch how much you share with a new man about your past. Don't fake like you're Wonder Woman, just side-step any topics you aren't proud of until that man gains your trust by proving that he's not the type to throw shit in your face.

The Mindset of Men Who Sell Dreams

Let's break down how to defend your ears from a man that wants to take advantage of your Disney Princess fantasy. The first step is a continuation of what was written above, you must watch what you give away to a man you're just getting to know! I don't care how good of a listener you are, there has not been a woman built that doesn't have a conversation trigger that sends them off on an autobiographical rant. Men know women like to talk about themselves, so what do men do? Let them talk and talk and talk. When she comes up for air and asks him a question his only response is to swing it back to her again, because we as men don't want to open up, we just want to fuck and keep it moving. I've talked to women who have been in relationships for months and still had no clue who these men were beyond their sense of humor, hate of their baby mama, or angry political beliefs. Knowing that a man likes to make nasty jokes, wishes he would have used a condom with his last bitch, or that he believes the Republicans are working with the police to kill black men, doesn't mean you know him on a real level. Women fall in love with men that let them talk, faster than men that actually talk to them. Why do you like to talk so much, because you feel as if you don't get to express yourself normally. **No one wants to hear you out, and you're frustrated, so the moment someone asks you about you, your ego explodes.** You just spray verbal diarrhea in the ear of a man who doesn't say a word but, "Fa'real?" In return, you bond fast, and he gets the pussy within a few weeks under the pretense of, "It felt like I've known him forever." No, Basica, you haven't known him forever, you were just talking for forever, and got so caught up in the excitement that you forgot that your pussy should cost more than a few hours of conversation.

"I knew he was lying, I'm not dumb." You purposely fell for game that you knew was game... what the fuck does that make you then, a genius? **Too many women worry about what's being said and ignore what's being done.** A manipulative man is better at propaganda than Hitler, and as a result, a generation of women have been trained to get open off of texting as opposed to flowers. For example, I had a girl email me about my book *Ho Tactics* after she used it on her boyfriend. Using the psychology in those pages, she was finally able to get her man to treat her to a fancy date. In this email she said being taken out to an expensive restaurant made her feel wrong. This was a woman so used to being courted like a basic bitch, that it felt dirty to be taken out and treated. That's a direct result of men bonding with women based on words, not actions. Today's men don't have to take girls on dates. They don't have to be consistent with their communication. They don't have to be romantic. All they have to do is listen to her life story, spot her holes, tell a girl his future plans and how she's apart of them, and watch as the girl buys in.

The better a man looks, the sweeter his lies taste. Be honest, hearing that good-looking loser promise you the world, feels better than getting your ass ate. Telling a woman what he is going to do for her is easier than doing it, and it gets a man the same results! Growing up most of you heard family or friends who played the lottery say, "When I hit this number, I'm going to buy a car like this. And I'll get you one like that." Hopeless people love to mentally escape, and hopeless romantics are no exception. Dreaming becomes dangerous when you're doing it with your eyes open. Ladies, you want the fantasy, he knows you want the fantasy, so why are you getting gassed when guys tell you how special you are, how you two would make pretty kids, or how you're the type he would marry? Morning Emoji's aren't proof that he loves you. Wanting to cum in you isn't a down payment on an engagement ring. You have a fetish for fantasy, and even if you roll your eyes and don't believe him at first, you still hear him out, which means you are flawed. He sees this crack in your armor and will use it to get what he wants no matter how much you claim to be smarter than him. After enough talk, you will buy in to the lie because that lie is better than your lonely reality.

The solution is to watch what you give away to a man and also observe how he uses the things you do offer to bait you in. For example, it's okay to tell a guy you plan on starting a small business. If he comes in with all the things he can do for you, fine, let him talk. The talk is one thing, the action is another. If he keeps telling you about the people he can introduce you to but never does, don't bring it up, know that he's hustling your ears. The same thing goes for vacations he wants to take you on, activities he wants to do with you for the next date, etc... the moment a man has piled up at least two—*I want to do this for you*, claims and doesn't actually do it. Cut ties. He's a dream seller.

The Mindset of Dishonest Men

The overarching theme that you've undoubtedly figured out is to be honest with who you are internally no matter how uncomfortable it makes current Avatar in this game of life. As always, the defensive counter-response will be, "Men are dishonest too! They don't know who they are, or what they want, and send mixed signals!" Men know exactly what they want, and if you were paying attention instead of cheesing every time he texted you, you would know this. **Men lie and manipulate, but they will tell you who they are and what they are all about in so many words if you are brave enough to ask about their past.** For example, a man will tell you in confidence that he fucked a plus size woman for months only because she paid his rent. He will tell you how he believes females are all undercover hos and confess in a joking manner how he partied various girls out to prove his theory. Ask any man you date going forward or think back to any man you dated previously, even the habitual liars were honest when it came to sum up his feelings on women in general. Because those were other woman he played and not you, it makes you feel as if you're exempt. In your inside the box manner of thinking why would a man confess his game to a woman he's dating. His stories of opinions must put you above those basic women of his past, right? Wrong!

So many women want to fit in with men, and they laugh at these stories like, "These hos are dumb, bae!" You're not his bae, you're his next victim, idiot. **While**

you feel as if you're now in "the club" because he told you his secrets, you're not. When he fucks you and starts acting up, you will understand that those weren't past stories. He was revealing his current lifestyle and character! Men are not hard to figure out if you open your fucking ears and stop assuming that he thinks you're different from the last girl. Males will dry snitch all day long because in the end telling on himself won't stop the average thirsty chick from thinking she's the exception. Stop feeding your ego and realize you're in the same boat as every other woman.

The Mindset of Men Who Don't Need Your Sex

I remember when I first learned that saying, "No" to a girl was like female Viagra. It's insane, we as men spend so many years trying to get a girl to say "Yes," when in actuality, it comes even faster when you act as if you don't want it. Men today understand that women hate to be rejected. It's not just about turning down sex, throw them any curve and females react aggressively to change your mind. Women don't often ask or go for sex, they drop hints, or they use code words to let you know you have the green light. To pretend as if you don't get the hint, if you're uninterested, or to get her revved up and pull away will mind-fuck her to the extreme. No one likes to be rejected, but when you're dealing with a woman who isn't usually vulnerable, who's fake tough and internally vulnerable, her thoughts will race with questions and answers: He didn't go for sex because he doesn't think you're pretty. He didn't finish because something you said or did turned him off. He's not calling you the next day because he feels you were too easy. The list goes on all day because that fire of rejection can't be put out until the rejected woman proves to the man that she is worthy of his time, dick, attention, etc...

A girl can have a phone full of men trying to have sex with her, an inbox full of admirers, even a few guys at work flirting with her, but all it takes is for one random guy to act indifferent and her self-confidence deflates like year-old ass shots. **A large percentage of women have unaddressed Daddy Issues that have given them a complex where they obsessively want those that don't want them.** It shouldn't be about who wants or doesn't want you that determines your self-esteem, but when you lie about that problem instead of addressing it, those wounds never heal, they fester bad relationship after bad relationship until you are literally undateable. For men, this is great, because as soon as a weak woman tries to fake Spartan Up, all he has to do is check her with, "I never wanted you in the first place, you're basic." Then instead of being strong like she bragged about, she's up late asking her bff, "So why doesn't he want me, what's wrong with me, do you think I'm basic?" Fix your mental instabilities or stay the fuck out of the dating arena, because you will get slaughtered!

The best example of romantic genocide is the modern-day concept of "ghosting" or "falling back" which, for the unhip, is the concept of a guy suddenly disappearing or becoming unreachable out of the blue when you swore things were going great. This could be after sex or even when you've never had sex. It's a mental game that few women know how to handle let alone understand. Thousands of those that have come to me for advice have been suckered in by the *fall back game*, and the best way I can describe it is a form of instant depression mixed with unrelenting abandonment anxiety.

Men fall back because they know thirsty women will break the speed limit to catch them. **The greatest trick a manipulative man has ever performed is the Push & Pull.** Let me take you through a month in the life of a *Dicktician* aka a *User* aka plain old *Dick*... The Dicktician meets a woman that he likes, gets her number, and puts on the pressure to try and see her. This woman isn't acting the way Dick is accustomed to, meaning she is either being stingy with the pussy, wanting to be treated to broke-fancy shit like Olive Garden dates, or generally giving attitude like she's the Joseline Hernandez of this reunion and has other options. Dick doesn't like uppity females that think they are powerful or should be treated to things. After a few weeks of this behavior, Dick falls back. He doesn't call her as much, he becomes short in his responses and acts as if he's generally annoyed. Dick spends the next week ducking direct questions about, "What's wrong," because there is nothing wrong. He may use excuses about work, family, or general stress to make it seems like it's not you, but him. This is the Push stage. Dick is gambling that you will become so stressed over this rejection that you humble herself and falls in line. No demands about dates. No stress to return calls. No more questions about where the relationship is going. You're declawed by the fear of this distance growing and this man you like abandoning you. In most cases, The Push works. The girl now blows up his voicemail and text messages with apologies, threats, more apologies, and finally begging. Once a weak bitch starts to beg, Dick realizes that he's won the battle. All of these ultimatums she was talking about, the dates she wanted, the time she demanded, she still wants... but she knows better than to ask now. She feels lucky to have him in her life, and the Dicktician knows this, and will now exploit her going forward.

A woman who gives into this thinks she's smarter than Dick, she believes that once he comes back and is made happy, she can then hook him and get what she wants. She thinks that his return is really her win. Wrong! Dick is already two steps ahead because he does this with EVERY FEMALE. Insecure girls aren't mentally prepared to deal with the Push & Pull. Dick will wait for this woman to act up again, and the moment she shows sign of being feed up or wanting to change him, he pulls away again, this time for a longer stretch. He didn't have to brag about his Fall Back Game being strong, he proved it with his actions, and that insecure woman played right into his hands. Pull-Push-Pull-Push, you can't stop it unless you confess that you have a problem with abandonment, an unrealistic need to be loved, and take steps to rectify those emotions.

Remember your Spartan Training from my previous books! You can't ever see a man as priceless to the point where you allow this reverse psychology hustle to drive you insane. The moment a man falls back, stop contacting him. One of two things will happen. He will stay away because he realizes that you're on to his hustle or he will come sniffing around with a random text message, "Hey stranger, I was just thinking about you." Don't reach out if he doesn't come sniffing around, I don't care how much chemistry you felt you had, how rich he is, or how epic his sex was. Don't respond to any random reach out. Leave his text message on "read" or leave his email unanswered. Ignore his social media tags and if you happen to run into him keep it quick and cordial. Weak women are easily lured back by basic attempts to reconnect because deep down they want to be wanted. Not a Spartan!

Typical or Unicorn

Now that you know some of the key personality traits to look out for, will you use it in your actual life? I doubt it. As long as there are other women to compare yourself to, you won't seek help or initiate change. Your pride keeps you locked into the mortal mind and unable to advance to Goddess consciousness. You'll feel empowered for a bit then you will point to other women who don't seem to need help or who are exceptions to the rule, and if they can win, you ignorantly believe you can keep stumbling through life and win as well. Ego Alert! If you were truly unique, then you would have addressed your issues, plugged the holes in your personality, and evolved into a true Spartan Queen that moves two steps ahead of these men, instead of a weak bitch that wanders around confused and angry. You care what men think about you—own that. You care when you don't get called back—own that. You worry that you won't find someone special—own that. You secretly feel that you aren't good enough to get the things you want—own that.

Delusion must die a painful death, and what's left will be the character you call "self" all alone with nothing but the hard-cold truth. I want you to go to that vulnerable place and stand naked with your thoughts until you can admit that you do typical things. When you see girls making comments on social media about no good men, and you find yourself constantly agreeing with them, it's because you're both common in your mindset. The same way she got played, you get played. Why is that? Because even a thousand miles apart, you do the same basic shit and fall for the same basic game! You pride yourself on being something out of the ordinary, but your personality is about as exotic as having blue eyes in Finland. A unique woman isn't sitting in the same boat with basic bitches, swapping war stories about the struggle.

A special woman can't relate with, "Yup, that's how men do you, girl!" because men don't pull that bullshit on special women.

The more you advance mentally, the less in common you have with the Tina Typicals of the world. The more you keep it real with yourself, the less you have in common with the bitter Basicas of the world. The more you understand yourself, the more you recognize which men are worth your time and what men are Dick just trying to waste your time. The path to being generic is easy, just keep pretending you're hot shit and that all your bad breaks are the result of others. The path to being great is hard because it forces you to tear down the safety net of your little girl ego, confront the ugly side of your personality, and address the traumatic side of your past. Stop lying, stop waiting, stop running, stop being content with being good enough and start growing into greatness.

Self-Therapy

How to Reset & Reclaim

*Y*ou now feel empowered. You're ready to go out and be a Spartan. Prove to yourself and the world that you're not basic nor do you behave like a typical love-starved woman. The problem is, when you walk outside, you freeze. The words about mastering your power fade. The strategy about how to vet men, what to look out for in terms of red flags, it all bleeds together. Your confidence once again plummets, and your Universe transforms into a scary world where you have no control. Why doesn't my writing stick? Why doesn't any empowering speech or inspirational video you consumed stick? You can read all day, leave reviews on what you loved and hated, but why don't you do anything in those books? It's easy to hide behind a keyboard and have opinions or theories about what works and what doesn't. It's hard to put it to the test because you actually have to go outside and engage with others. Basic women never take actions because internally they are still anchored by fear of failure. It's time to be a driver, not a passenger. Self-therapy is the key that will bridge the gap between reading and nodding along and reading and going out into the world to win. I have years of positive results from real men and women who used my books to change their fate. Doesn't matter the age, race, or country of origin. Once the fear is carved out, your power to attract at the highest level begins. This chapter is about taking control in a practical way. No one makes it to adulthood without sustaining some form of emotional damage. Let's not run away from that any longer, let's run towards it.

Who hurt you and why can't you let it go? Your childhood wasn't ideal, how much pity do you need to move forward from that? Your first time loving someone ended with betrayal, how much anger and regret needs to build up before you get over it? No one appreciates what you do for them, how many times do you need to keep pointing that out before you stop being unselfish? 9 out of 10 people are never going to change they're just going to complain. Hurt feels like armor at first, it keeps you safe, but it's actually a cage that stunts you emotionally and poisons every choice you make. You love being petty, you love bringing up the past, you love having an attitude, you get off on reminding people about all you do for them, and you really love shifting blame for your mediocre life onto someone else. That's your safe place–reminding people that nothing is your fault because being a victim feels better than the admission that you have no idea of how to do better.

Let's define what it means to be damaged. I'm referring to those that have been traumatized by people or events, and instead of seeking to come to grips with those things, they continue as if nothing is wrong. Ignorantly allowing those wounds to fester, spread, and turn them into a shell of their former self. All of this happens in silence, it's a form of depression that works under the surface then rears its ugly head the moment they try to connect, trust, or love someone new. You don't want someone to turn back around and hurt you after you've already explained your pain, so you settle into this little bubble where you remain guarded and miserable. I guarantee that more than half the people reading this pretend they're not bothered in public then cry into their pillow in private. It's time to talk about these mental issues instead of faking like everyone is so tough well put together.

Damage Checklist: You complain about shit from the past that you can't change. You distract yourself with whatever dumb ass news story that's dominating social media. You self-medicate with shopping, drugs, or drink. You claim to be over everything and everybody...but that doesn't stop you from letting the same types of people that hurt you before right back into your life to hurt you again. One day you're blessed and highly favored, the next day you're crying about how things will never work out for you. Now be honest. You're not random, you're depressed and have no idea of how to shake those hot and cold moments. Life forges you like fucking steel, not so you can be hard and cold, but so you can cut through the bullshit. Yet, life's lessons are lost on you as you recycle exes, fall in love with obvious liars, let shady family and friends continue to manipulate you, and point the finger outward instead of dusting your weak ass off and taking a stand! **This universe is built to help those that help themselves, and the first rule of ascending is don't expect another human to play fair.** The reason why I'm so loud has nothing to do with me and everything to do with you all. To see an intelligent woman, make a dumb decision over a dick that isn't even hers is a waste. To see a stand-up guy, turn towards misogynistic views because he can't deal with a woman's rejection is a waste. All of you have the potential to be happy and to rise above your past, but you keep slipping back into the bullshit because you're afraid to truly work on yourself.

Just because you're damaged doesn't mean you're broken. If you're single, it feels hopeless when you realize that for anyone to love you they will have to learn you, and when your past is filled with mistakes, you wonder who would want that. If you're in a relationship that's struggling it feels as if the only option is to put up with it because who else would accept you in your current state except for the devil you know. Stop feeding into negativity and regain faith in yourself. There is nothing wrong with you that can't be fixed over time and no trauma that can't be healed with self-love. Life may not have given you the results you were expecting, but that doesn't mean your story can't change overnight. Don't say "*I deserve better*" mean that shit! **If you lie to yourself long enough, being comfortable starts to feel the same as being happy—but it's not real.** Do you truly love yourself or are you just stuck in a body living a life that you can't change so you make do? Laugh at celebrities because that makes you forget about your own flaws. Get enraged about politics because that helps you channel your own self-hatred somewhere else. Plop your ass in front of a screen and watch a TV show, because watching fiction helps you numb your facts. Here's an idea... Instead of avoiding all your issues let's lift that rug where you've hidden all the things you're ashamed of and start to glue your life back together.

Addicted to The Same Type

"Why are men always lying about dumb shit?" Um, why do you continue to talk to men that consistently lie in the first place? I notice a pattern with women when they complain about Fuck Boys, they talk around the real problem. A girl would rather question why a man acts the way he acts then question why she's attracted to a man that consistently acts in that fucked up manner. If I own a cat that scratches at me every time I go to pet it, I'm getting rid of the fucking cat, not psychoanalyzing why it's being an asshole. **Damaged women are attracted to flawed men as if being emotionally unavailable is Maca Root.** The core of this attraction, from the people I've studied, is that a woman feels that if she works hard to understand why a man treats her like shit, he'll repay that compassion by doing the same investigation into her issues.

Let's keep it real, you wish you had someone who was brave enough to sit you down and ask why you're hurting. You wish a man cared enough to try and understand and fix you, so you pour all this love into their problems hoping it's reciprocated...but it never is. You waste all your time and energy on a guy that either runs off with another girl or is content to have you waiting around until he decides if he wants more. You rebuild a man for the next bitch, ensuring that he now understands how to now be a good boyfriend, meanwhile whose left to rebuild you? This leaves you stuck crying about how good you were to someone that's off being Mr. Perfect for his next woman. When you find the energy to finally move on and try to love once more, guess who gets your pussy throbbing next? The same type of man!

How can you vent about needing a "Russell Wilson Type" when those type of men don't even get your nipples hard? Look at the last four guys you really liked, I bet you they all had more in common than not. Look at the last four guys you didn't feel chemistry with, I bet they had their shit together emotionally. *He's corny, he's a nerd, it's just something about him.* Yeah, that something is called, *"Being too secure."* **Dating someone that has their shit together only points out just how far behind your own life is.** Have you ever seen a young person be given a job above an older person? They resent them on the surface but what's really going on is that they resent themselves for still being their age and not as far along—it's the same thing with damaged people trying to date a person who isn't insecure, a constant self-loathing reminder! The easy fix is to pursue someone who will allow you to play make believe, someone either worse off than you or that needs fixing. That shit never works, and you're left bogged down with someone else's problems while yours grow and grow.

Another piece of this fucked up mental puzzle is the want to prove and validate your past through the men of your present. Damaged women are constantly chasing the ex that hurt them or the man that rejected them because through conquering a man like her shitty boyfriend or absentee father she can prove to herself that it wasn't her—it was him. The problem becomes that when you pick men with those traits, you're skipping over the clear fucking message of—stay away from men like that you idiot! **Your head's hard and your pussy is moist, so you end up riding the dick of a guy that pushes you away and pulls you back in only to push you away again, and you end up calling that "true love."** You're not dumb, you know these things, you just refuse to articulate them. You see a guy on Instagram that has the same dumb ass haircut as your boyfriend from two years ago, and you automatically like him for a reason you don't tie together. You go to a bar and flirt with a guy that has the same smart-ass sense of humor as the guy that fucked you and never called you again, and you automatically feel a spark for a reason you don't tie together. Get the picture yet? You're not woke to your own toxic attractions, you're sleepwalking through life because you refuse to admit you have a problem choosing men.

Your hormones are locked onto those with a high chance of shitting on you, but when someone asks why you're single you respond with some basic bitch slogan like: _Because boys suck_! No, beloved, the boys you try to turn into men suck because you equally suck. You break up, blame the guy for acting the way guys like him act, and then rush back on the market to repeat this step. Pump your breaks! Stop dating for a minute. Stop taking phone numbers. Stop responding to DMs. Understand what you're chasing after because it's not male love. You're driven by the lack of self-love tied to something that hurt you in your childhood or adolescence, and that needs to be healed before you start dating again.

Assuming Everyone
Wants to Play You

Another type of damaged woman is the one that is overly cautious and full of attitude. I get emails from a handful of women that will run down a normal date then always end it with, *"So what do you think? He's trying to play me, right?"* You want someone to co-sign your paranoia because you're deathly afraid of going through heartbreak again. You can't spend life in a shell! Men want pussy—who doesn't know that? Should men not want to fuck you? A part of falling for a woman is first being sexually attracted to her, you can't get one without the other, and anyone that tries to blow smoke up your ass about how he fell in love with your mind first is lying. Kill all this noise about not wanting a man that objectifies you and wanting someone that's "just a friend" because you sound naïve. I get it, a man led you on then fell back. A boyfriend broke up with you after he got all the benefits of your unselfish behavior. A guy who said he wasn't like the rest treated you just like the rest, and you're sick of crying over men. You think the solution is to throw on your Savage mask, turn Cardi B up, and live a life where you fuck these men before they fuck you—but you're not built like that, cupcake. You think the solution is to avoid dating, focus on work or school, and buy a case of batteries—but you still lust for love, princess. **If you sit out the game for fear of being injured how many championships do you think you'll win?** People are sneaky and devious, but you can't tell me that any woman that's read the majority of this website or any of my books can't outwit a player or see through a mindfuck in a week or less? Being damaged isn't just about the obvious bad behavior or funky attitude, it's also about being so stuck in your fear that you refuse to give anyone a chance. You don't have to ask me, your friends, or google if someone is out to get you—assume they are but go into battle knowing that you're a fucking Spartan, and no dick tactics formed against you can possibly penetrate your mental armor!

Chasing After Rejection

The saddest sign that a woman needs to do self-healing and awaken her inner Spartan is when she chases after a man that's making it clear he doesn't want her. At least twice a week I get asked, *"Do you think he likes me,"* then presented with evidence where a woman should already know that he doesn't. The dating stage is complicated, it relies on signs and assumptions. You can text all week with someone or go out on a long date and feel as if they get you, then the next week they switch up on you, leaving you confused. I've covered in exhaust how people put on fronts during the honeymoon stage of getting to know a person and that only through time and patience can you truly be sure of an agenda. Still, when you're hurting and looking for a savior in the form of a lover, it's hard to see the writing on the wall. You're expecting him to not call you after sex—but he does like nothing has changed only to fall back before having sex again. He takes you out on three dates, you don't have sex, and he seems as if he likes you even more than you like him—but he falls back. Everything is going good, you think this is about to be official—but he stops texting you with the same enthusiasm, and he doesn't make plans to see you as he once did. Talk about confusing! All of these rules you try to follow are turned upside down, and you don't know why this keeps happening to you. Instead of accepting that his falling back is proof of incompatibility, you try to win him back, and that's where you ruin your life.

A man will reject you in such a subtle yet obvious way that every part of you will refuse to accept it. The ego hates to be humbled, so it reaches for an excuse that will make the rejection sting less. You want to learn how men think. You want to backtrack to see what could have gone wrong. You want to stalk his social media to see if he found someone else. You want to text him paragraphs asking what you did wrong. You want to call and say, "Fuck you, clown! You ain't all that anyway!" These thoughts race through your head, but the truth is you just want someone to like you or give you another chance to show that you are likable. When you have gone through various men falling back multiple times, each new rejection reminds you that you aren't what guys are looking for. It's not just one or two men—every man that has gotten to know you has shown that. Even when they come back trying to talk to you again, it ends the same way, so the victory of "they always *come back*," is meaningless. Those guys didn't return because they felt as if you were special, they are either bored or gaming. What hurts more, a man that comes back and plays you or going out and meeting a new guy that doesn't live up to his potential? You all want the comfort of that old thing, but you fail to notice that by being constantly rejected by a person that knows you intimately it does more damage. How many times are you going to let him come over late at night for a talk that turns into his face between your legs? How many times are you going to unblock him hoping the bullshit he texts you is any different from the last time? How many times are you going to let someone keep sampling you only to remind you that you're not good enough?

Knowing how males think won't make one take you back. Texting a man paragraphs on top of paragraphs about your feelings won't make him reconsider you as the wifey type. Unfollowing a man on social media won't make him call you. Posting a meme about *"They always want you after you find someone else,"* will not inspire remorse. Going to go fuck your ex or some random that happens to be around won't send a message that he's missing out. If a man wants you, he goes all in to get you! There doesn't need to be outside pressure or blackmail to make him see you for what you as special! He either does, or he doesn't. If he's not showing love, he's not feeling love—it's just that simple!

How it feels when we are into a woman:

She doesn't have to text you first, you reach out whenever she's on your mind. Even when you're busy, you find time to see her. You give without expecting anything in return. You don't reach out exclusively at night when you want pussy. You don't leave things unsaid when you know she's upset for any reason. You don't have her wondering what you are, you tell her she's yours!

You can't check any of those things off your list because the men you're crying about don't fucking want you. Nevertheless, you play yourself by continuing to reach out until he's forced to respond. If and when he responds what happens next? **A man's lies are as strong as fentanyl in the ears of a weak woman.** He calms you down with a "sorry" or a lame excuse as to why he's been acting that way. You forgive him, let him back in for as long as he's bored or on break from the life he would rather be living, then he pulls the same trick. He pushed you away because he didn't want you the way you wanted him, you pulled him back because you hated to be rejected, did you think that was going to last? Reaching back out or being receptive to you reaching out again doesn't prove shit but the presence of boredom or horniness. "*My friend got back with this guy that was playing games, now they have a kid together and are happy,*" turns into, "*Remember my friend, her baby daddy broke up with her for another girl, why are guys so fucked up!*" Someone really told me that, and all I could do is laugh. Of course he left her because she forced a relationship on a man that didn't want her. It happens every single day and dudes will always find an escape route because no one wants to stay with a Placeholder!

You're so damaged and desperate that you deny this truth in favor of the narrative that he manipulated you. No Basica, the snake fell to the ground and slithered away, you ran through the grass looking for the snake because you don't have any other options, and he bit your ass. Don't be bitter, be better! Your insecurities made you fall for the type of treatment that a more powerful woman would have never put up with, so what separates your gullibility from her wisdom? You have yet to do the real work to find out why your emotional holes won't close. Let's go there.

Stop Hating, Start Healing

Somewhere in your life story there is an incident or setback that you're clinging to that continues to hold you back and you're the only one that can pull that out. You can talk to your mother or father. You can track down an ex on Facebook and have closure. You can get surgery to be more visually appealing. You can get straight A's or amass a huge savings account... none of that is going to stomp out the way you feel about yourself. The fake smile you call "life" needs to be wiped away so you can finally admit that you're not happy living this way. There is nothing so horrible that you can't recover from it! I've seen women get incurable STDs, regroup and still find love. I've helped women that have gone through sexual abuse rise above and remember their power. I've talked to several women that had men they considered to be soulmates die, and each one bounced back once they stopped cursing their circumstances. You must find the courage to dig into whatever you hate about your life and address that because no one else will ever care enough to do it for you.

Go Inside, Every Day: I've noticed something in my travels. For all the new age books, crystals, vision boards, or whatever that a lot of you are into, many people don't even know how to meditate. Literally, you can't sit in a room alone and go inside your own head for 20 minutes. I'm not surprised because most can't even properly shit unless they're scrolling a timeline. This ADD way of living is the core of why you don't get anywhere emotionally. **You're always talking, always reacting, always doing detective work. When do you have time to stand still and think?** The key to being happy alone, and not just faking it, is to learn to become your own best friend, your own mentor, and your own therapist.

I want you to start with 15 minutes a day and build your focus until you can go for 20 or 30 minutes a day. Isolate yourself from other people, electronics, and your normal way of thinking. None of you are so busy that you can't take time in the morning or at night before bed to sink into nothing. You don't have to cross your legs or do some specific breathing exercise. Start by getting to the point where you can sit still for that first five minutes. If you have an idea, remember a bill that needs to be paid, or start fixating on not thinking, catch yourself, empty it out, and focus on the blackness of your closed eyelids. Don't try to tap into some higher thought or figure out your problems. Just relax. Be nothing.

The next step is to ask yourself everything that's hidden from the character you play. This isn't about love advice, this is about life in general. Do you really like your parents? Do your current group of friends know the real you or just the mirage? What can't you stand about your present life? What's really making you mad when you get into moods? What deep secret are you holding in; did you steal when you were younger, cheat, lie? Is the job you're at really what you want to be doing? Are you lazy? Are you fake? Are you sexually frustrated? Are you the type of person you would want to be friends with? Eventually, you'll land on *"why haven't I found love."* In the privacy of your own head, where you can admit anything without penalty, it will be time to answer that with the truth, not the excuse. Replay this exercise at least five days a week. I guarantee you that by the third week you will have discovered stuff about yourself that will make you take ownership of your life choices.

No Date Zone: All the guys you date, even the ones that were good eggs, didn't work out. What did they have in common? Why did you agree to be exclusive? What were the things that bothered you about them? What were the things that bothered them about you? The goal is to stop jumping into relationships just because it's expected and ask yourself why do you even need a relationship at this point in your life? What can that person bring to your table? What path are you on, and is it better to be solo? Sex is great, having someone to talk about your day with is amazing, but those things aren't more important than personal goals. Some lives revolve around other people making them happy, while others know that it's about making self happy.

There's nothing wrong with turning your nose up at the status quo of "You must have someone to be happy." If anything, shrugging off this idea that you need external love, is necessary for developing emotional maturity. The old you, that weak chick that got stuck on crushes and took every rejection to heart will fade away once you realize it's not that serious. That old you, the soft guy that always chose the wrong women will crumble once you realize that you don't have to chase to attain. How do you start over? You don't just pump your breaks, you park the car and fix all that crap built up under your hood.

Could you go on a romantic fast even in the face of pursuit by the type of people you would normally date? Is your discipline that strong that you could curve some good looking dude who approaches you? If not, here are a few tips: <u>What do you do when someone tries to get your number?</u> You take it, but you don't use it. Put it in the "hey stranger" jar for possible use when you're back in the game. <u>What do you do when someone from the past who you always crushed on gets in contact with you?</u> You keep it friendly but decline any social outing or attempt to creep into your life. Don't be consumed with this thought of "*what if this is the one.*" You're brainwashing yourself to go back out there before you're ready under some superstitious ideology that opportunity only knocks once. **If that person is the one for you, they'll always be the one for you.** A fast is a fast. No dating. No texting. No hanging out as if it's not a date. Deal with what you need to. Heal. Live life free of the stress of relationships. Get your life in the order you want emotionally or financially. This could take a month, or it could take a year. Only you know how much time alone you truly need. The goal is to be disciplined enough to let what seems like a perfect pitch glide pass you. You can't become clear of thought until you're free of distractions and rid of this pressure to belong to someone.

Stop Being Bitter: Ever talk to someone that was single for a year or more? Hell, maybe you are that person who has been single for a year or more. Not to generalize, but most of the women who come to me fitting that description have horrible attitudes, negative dispositions, and they wear excuses like body lava. They know everything about dating and relationships, and in their opinion, everyone is playing games, all men cheat, all girls are hos, and anyone that's happy is fronting. When you question them on their own inability to find love, they point you to the city they live in full of bums. They point you to the type of women guys pick over them, "*all these guys say they want someone real, but they chase after these Dr. Miami bitches.*" They're high opinionated about everything except for one-touch subject—their past. 9 out of 10 women who come to me for advice finally cave in and all that hot air deflates as I force them to tell me about their father who wasn't there, that mother who put others before them, or the ex that had her looking stupid.

That anger, that sour taste, that hate they spew under cover of "love is dumb," is a shield meant to hide the fact that they can't figure out why no one actually wanted them at any stage of life. No one will ever choose you for you. Think about that. It hurts. But it's not true, and that's what I need you Forever Single chicks to over-stand.

One girl would always write me about what her friend was doing and how dumb she was for not seeing through these users. I told her to drop her opinions about her friend and focus that shit inward because she and her BFF were one in the same. Both women were looking for validation because of rough childhoods, both women got excited anytime a new dick tried to date her, both women swore off love once they got fucked and ghosted. She wasn't single because she was taking a break. She was single because unlike her friend, she stayed in the house most times, mean mugged when out, and didn't have anyone willing to approach that toxic energy she was emitting. Whereas her friend was more carefree and extroverted. After I pointed that out, she snapped back with her size as a reason why men don't approach her. See how deflection works? Her weight didn't make her unattractive, her friend was just as big as she was, and was having success on that shallow level of being pulled. It was her disposition that made her ugly. I told her all of this, and she fell back from wanting my advice... until she ended up fucking some guy that was a new hire at work. Then she ran back to me crying about how he dogged her out and was now smashing some girl at work she hated.

Why was a woman like this who had been single for over three years so easy to be manipulated by the first new dick that winked at her? Because bitter people who have been single for too long don't know shit. They theorize and give opinions about love, but when it comes to putting all that sass and bombastic wisdom to the test, they get exposed as just another love-starved Basica. They never worked on "self" they just hardened and embraced a negative outlook, and neither of those things are healthy ways to unlock the path to Spartanhood.

If you're a woman who wags your finger, "*tell men they need to stop playing so many games,*" then you've already lost. **People will always do what they want. The solution isn't for Karma, God, or the fucking Easter Bunny to punish people into being nice, it's for you to recognize the game and expose the real from the fake.**

You're bitter because using your brain to expose people's intentions is too much work for your lazy ass. You're too tired to put in work, so you choose to stay single. The irony is that you will run into someone that wants something from you and once again be too lazy to even test their agenda. Your bitter hibernation didn't smarten you up to the hustle, you just folded your arms. Life is a game! You can't NOT play it, so get that stick out of your ass, fix your funky attitude, and smarten up to how to WIN, not how to complain.

Take Responsibility: You're not single because of your city. You're not single because of your looks. You're not single because all men are immature assholes. You have to stop throwing yourself a pity party. You picked the wrong person. Fact. You either knew they were wrong for you or missed signs and found out the hard way. Fact. You can either dwell in your past or move into the future with a better understanding of what happened. Fact! **Taking responsibility doesn't mean you admit that everything's your fault, stop being so dense. Taking responsibility is about regaining ownership of your life to take control of your future.** When you sit around and point point point, what does that do? The milk is spilled, the damage is done, and moving forward all you'll do is look back to how you were done dirty and use it to excuse your current lack of success. Are you that person that cries about being fired from a job and points to that as the reason why you can't get hired right now or are you that person that laughs about being fired from a job because it led to you getting something better? It's all about your outlook.

I have a buddy that got herpes from her ex-boyfriend. They were together for years, it wasn't perfect, but it was good most of the times. She had no idea that her "man" would bring something back to her. They broke up, and she came to me with a positive spin on how she was going to move forward. He was a flawed man. She knew he had holes in his character. She ignored them and accepted him. *"GL, that was my mistake for spending all that time with a man who acted sketchy more than once."* Some of you would probably sink into a deep depression and swear off love... you would literally allow someone to put a stop to your life. This woman didn't, she took that hand she was dealt, and rebuilt herself. She's now happily married with a man who accepted her for who she was. That's power, that's maturity, that's a fucking Spartan. You get knocked down, you don't cry about fairness, you internalize how you got knocked down, grow wiser, and move into that next chapter with a positive mindset that you will do better this time around.

Kill the Old You: Meditate. Ask those deep questions I outlined above. Most importantly, switch your POV so you can embrace real change. Unlike those that are coming off a breakup and retain some form of optimism, eternally single people have this wall of negativity built up towards life. It's not just love, being unhappy and alone has jaded you towards damn near every subject. You're like a walking one-star Yelp review, that's how salty you've allowed yourself to become. The solution is to try on the POV of Appreciation. Be thankful! Instead of pointing out everything wrong in this world. When you go to work and get annoyed, mellow yourself, and switch to that POV. When you see something that reminds you of how somebody did you dirty in a past relationship and just want to punch something, switch to that POV. Positive thinking, like meditation, is hard to master because few know how to do it. Stop trying to force happy thoughts and look on the bright side of "thanks." That inner hater will starve if you do this consistently for a month. That mean mug you put on will soften. The energy you're projecting to strangers and friends will improve. By the end of the month, you will then be able to look back and see that all that frustration and anger was pointless. The POV of Appreciation is your Phoenix Force, it will resurrect the part of you that the world buried.

There is nothing wrong with investing in external therapy sessions, talking to your true friends, or writing down all the ways where you feel weak or insecure, so you can set a goal to repair each of those areas day by day. The answer to moving towards who you were always meant to be starts with ridding yourself of the person that's been holding you back. When I look in the eyes of my newborn daughter these days, and she grins, there isn't any pain or worry. Each one of you was innocent until the world darkened you, and you owe it to yourself to find a way back to that place.

It's Going to Be Okay

All damage is curable, yes even the horrible thing that just popped into your head. You never fully get rid of past trauma. You make it into a part of you. A positive aspect where you can point to your head and say, "I survived impossible odds, I'm a warrior Queen!" In order to get to that point where your battle scars are badges of honor, you need to patiently rebuild your self-esteem and gently remove all traces of guilt. For this kind of therapy to happen, you need time alone. Being single can be the best thing to ever happen to your mental health if you spend that time addressing all the things you need to work on as opposed to dwelling on past relationships or anticipating future ones. Is your money right? Are your career goals being met? Are you having fun in life or are you living just to pay bills and waste time online? The lie you've been sold is that you need someone else to come into your world and make your life better by loving you unconditionally. External love is often fleeting and rarely unconditional, people give and take their love away, and you have no control over that. Focus on being great enough for you, not good enough for some flavor of the week! Stop using the time between relationships to sit on your ass and complain and start to constructively build the kind of life you want to be living regardless of who is or isn't in it.

The Unicorn Delusion:

The right person will always come into your life at the right time, but you're so wrapped up in waiting for them that you're neglecting the fact that you aren't yet right in your own life. Stop talking about your aspirations, stop over-planning your next move, stop with any excuse that has you standing still instead of moving forward. Spoiler Alert: Working on yourself, takes actual work! There is nothing that can hold you back from rebounding from a bad breakup. Trust issues, low self-esteem, past betrayals, present hopelessness, the fear of a future where you'll always be alone—You can beat all of those things once you master emotional maturity! Help yourself to heal by giving yourself the proper time to heal. Once you come out of the fog, start to re-engage slowly. Date casually, so you won't relapse into the pressure to find a boyfriend. If you're horny, have sex casually, so you won't relapse into the crutch of liking someone based on the physical. Pace yourself as if it's your first time learning to ride a bike. Be sure the damage that had you out here looking foolish is truly rectified before you fully immerse yourself in any romantic goals. Most importantly, don't stop your daily routine of self-therapy, it will keep you emotionally honest and mentally sharp.

By G.L. Lambert

Solving Single Bonus Chapter

Dating When You Don't Want a Serious Relationship

*B*eing single doesn't always translate into being unwanted. We live in an era where it seems every girl on social media is waiting up for some mythical, "him" and upgrading a Facebook status from single is greeted with dozens of likes and congratulations as if that's a milestone. In "realer" life it's the one question everyone from your grandmother to your OB/GYN makes small talk about—are you dating anyone? Your relationship status does not define you but everywhere you turn, it seems to be the thing on which you're constantly judged. Settle dick uses this relationship craze to prey on those women who fear being alone forever. Rival females use it to rattle your ego as if you're less desirable than they are because they "keep a man." Compliments about being too pretty to be alone, warnings about being too picky to ever find a man, or backhanded comments pointing to how you selfishly ignore the nice guys who are right under your nose; these are the verbal jabs people use to break down those girls who turn down date offers with, "No thanks, I'm doing me right now."

I've found that it's not the men that chip away the most at a woman's relationship insecurities, but other females. The moment a braggadocios girl finally gets a man, she feels the need to look down on women who are still single. Two weeks into a relationship (that she had to beg for with a guy she most likely wasn't into at first) and a Basic Bitch is suddenly a relationship expert who knows all about "good man" trapping. This type of girl can't wait to tell you what you're saying wrong, point out the flaws in your wardrobe, and then try to push you on her boyfriend's lame ass cousin, as if you aren't capable of finding a mediocre dick on your own. For some women it's not enough to find a man for themselves; they have to further prove their greatness by finding one for every girl in the crew. It's amazing how men and women alike can't comprehend that there are females who are genuinely happy in life and don't need a man texting, calling, and taking her to out to feel special.

Single isn't a dirty word, but people in the 21st century are more embarrassed by being single than being poor. I've seen people laugh and joke about being unemployed or working a low paying job because it's not shameful if the people you know are struggling financially as well, it's normal. However, when it comes to relationship status I've seen women give excuses to complete strangers to explain why they don't have a boyfriend or husband. You can explain being a college graduate waiting tables at Outback on the economy but in their insecure minds, they can't explain being a decent looking female who doesn't have a man. Not everyone who is in a relationship feels complete, and not everyone who's single feels lonely. Nevertheless, like my alcoholic 8th grade English teacher used to slur, "*No man a' island*," Meaning that we all need human interaction, or we'll go crazy. There will come a time where you will have to find someone who can fulfill that need for real love and romance, but in the meantime, there are certain itches that need to be scratched as well.

How do you fulfill your needs physically or emotionally when you aren't in a position to give your all to a man? A woman in college is focused on securing her degree, and while she likes to unwind on the weekend, she doesn't have the energy to deal with the boys on campus who want to be up under her 24-7. A career woman just starting out wants to make an impression, so she throws herself into her job, no time to entertain the various guys who want to talk her ear off after work or hog her weekends. Let's not forget about the single mom who has to juggle motherhood with paying the bills. Guys want to pay for babysitters and take her out, but maybe she's not ready to split her focus on a third entity. Then we have the party girls who just want to turn up six days out of the week without having to answer to a jealous man. Finally, there are those women who have been heartbroken or have some major personal issues that they need to figure out before they jump back in that pool. These "damaged" girls always meet prospects, but they aren't in the right mindset to give a man the type of love he wants, so they smartly decline close encounters. Love will find everyone eventually, but it takes a shrewd and seasoned woman to realize that there is no shot clock when it comes to romance.

Don't get me wrong, making a man get in where he fits in can be done and nearly every woman will have to juggle love, life, and career at some point in her life. Nevertheless, you shouldn't feel that it's your duty to split your focus to accommodate a man for the sake of saying you have a man. Skeptics will say that any girl who claims not to want a relationship is just scared to get played, but it's not always about hurt;

some females have the discipline to put self-improvement before romance. I've spoken to many women who realized that they weren't in a position to be a girlfriend first and live their own lives second. Is that selfish of them? Yes, and women who practice this behavior should pat themselves on the back because for far too long females have been made to think being selfish is a sin. This is Sparta, and you will always come first!

Countless men, past and present, have kept women at a distance while they figured their shit out, earned their fortune, or pursued their higher education. These men weren't scolded or shamed because they had no time for traditional love. Society labeled that behavior as a man "finding himself" or "making his way in life." When the fuck is a woman supposed to find herself? When is a woman supposed to make her way in life? From high school onward, it has been *get a boyfriend, keep a boyfriend, and wait for the ring.* Once again, gender roles have become a noose which women are still being strangled with in the 21st century. Your life should never revolve around getting a boyfriend or finding a husband, the primary goal is becoming a great individual that pulls other great individuals into their atmosphere. Even still, the need for love and companionship can't be ignored regardless of your reason for taking a break from relationships. A part of you will always long for male interaction on more than that platonic level. Girls have told me bluntly that sometimes they need dick, and the vibrator just isn't enough. Others have said that they're fine not having sex, but it would be nice to have someone to cuddle with that doesn't have a vagina. Some girls want the reward without the risk, and if dudes can milk the cow for free, chicks can ride the bull without having to buy the beef. In ratchet terms, *bitches want to have their cake and eat it too,* and I think they have that right. **This chapter will get into the ins and outs of dating when you're not looking for a serious relationship, just an outlet.** While the average person may laugh and say that women have a nasty habit of catching feelings when it's supposed to be emotionless, I do believe it can be achieved. It's not about cutting off your emotions or seeing men only as meat; it's about being disciplined enough to get what you want out of the situation, and then let go once that itch has been scratched.

The Girl Who Just Wants Sex

You want to fuck; not make love, not have sex, but fuck like an animal when the feeling rushes over you. The problem is that you don't want to be seen as a slut, a ho, catch a disease, or get your business aired out by the guy you're smashing on the weekends. Welcome to the world of man, ladies. It may seem that guys don't really care about whom they stick their dicks in, but they're more selective than you think, sometimes too selective. There are men who court jumpoff pussy as actively as they court girlfriends, which is the top reason girls get confused as to what a man wants (as if he should be an asshole instead of a gentleman if he only wants sex from you). Those slutty men who you are disgusted by are merely the sloppy ones you know about because they do put their sexual business in the street. However, there are numerous men who aren't looking for anything serious and aren't sloppy. Unlike boastful little boys, these men move in silence, are polite, respectful, and keep the entire relationship private. The messy aspect of males, even the gentlemen, who initiate this type of pact, is that they often lead women on instead of being forthcoming about what they want due to the fear that girls won't willingly agree to be pussy. As a result, guys slide into a sex only relationship with girls who assume it's going somewhere real. Women can secure a sexual relationship easier and more honestly than men can, but only if they throw caution, shyness, and fear of rejection to the wind.

A girl I email with told me that she just wants a delivery penis, no watching movies in her crib, no cooking dinner, just a guy to come over and fuck her after *Scandal* goes off. The problem was that she didn't know how to initiate this kind of relationship. "I can't just walk up to a cute guy and say 'let's fuck,' he'd think I was crazy!" Stop making things so dramatic, ladies. This isn't about walking up to a stranger and telling him that his height and smile turn you on and you want to go fuck in the coat check room. No one outside of a Taiwanese whorehouse is that forward when it comes to sex. Realistically you don't want to have sex with a stranger you just met because there is no trust. One night stands are a different kind of monster, random, spontaneous, and understood as a one and done deal. If your goal is to have a penis on call, it does take a bit of effort. Given that he's going to be a big part of your life, you should interview that man you want to sex the same way you would interview a guy that wants to be your boyfriend.

You're literally putting your life and reputation in a guy's hands. You should know basic things about his personality, even if it is "just sex." If he's the type that sees you as more than pussy and wants you to be his girl, he's not going to settle for, "I'm, doing me right now," and be happy renovating your walls, eventually he's going to get in his feelings and act out like a stereotypical female would. Know that man, even if all you want is his penis! There have been guys who've posted pictures on Twitter as payback for not getting what they want, exposed secret relationships on Facebook long after the FWB situation ended, and I personally know a dude who lied about having a condom on and got a girl pregnant because she only saw him as dick. Men are just as psycho as women are if they're rejected emotionally. Don't believe that all men fit into the, "I'm cool with just sex" box, interview his ass. He looks good, and that's the kind of guy whose face you want to ride like a Kawasaki, there's nothing wrong with that, but remember that good-looking guys aren't rare. You may have to pass up light eyes at the bar because he shows signs of being overly romantic, but rest assured that you will meet someone just as attractive the next time you're out dick scouting, and he may be a better candidate for lunchtime quickies where you don't have to cuddle after. The key is to be selective, aggressive, and most importantly have the ability to communicate the arrangement that you want.

How to Initiate: There isn't a specific place you should go to meet guys who will be into fuck friend situations; the same way you meet men normally is the same way you should go about meeting these kind of boy toys. If you don't know where to meet men, then clearly you didn't read this book comprehensively. Go and start over from Chapter One, and don't stop until you understand how easy it is pull a man into your world. Once you do meet a guy that you are attracted to, don't be negative or self-defeating. Women tend to beat themselves up as if they don't look good enough to get the good-looking guys. Others make the mistake of avoiding men completely because they don't trust themselves NOT to fall in love. Some don't want to hurt the feelings of a man who wants to be hers exclusively, so they become social hermits. Trust that you look good enough to get any man hard, that no dick created can whip you, and that any man who signs up for what you are about to offer knows what he's getting into—no more excuses. Another negative thought will be, "he doesn't look like the type that would be into that." Bullshit, even nice guys like sex. I don't care if the guy that gets you moist is stumbled upon at church or at your son's little league practice, assume that he's down to beat the breaks off that emotionally unavailable pussy. Having the confidence that what you are bringing to the table won't be turned down is mandatory for success.

The rules remain the same as if you were looking for a friend to date or talk to; Flirt, exchange numbers, find time to meet up face to face, and see if he's someone you actually like and trust. This is the most important step. Do not be impulsive and ask a guy on the phone the day after the first time you meet if he's down to be your dick daddy. By not vetting him properly, you may end up with a creep who ends up posting your panties on Instagram. Take your time and be sure that he's right for you, this isn't a race and you aren't just giving your box away, he has to be worthy enough to fuck. Unlike boyfriend hunting, this should be much more seductive and sexually charged. Put it on Front Street early on that you aren't looking for a man currently and let him react. He may be someone who is looking for a girl to settle down with, and that lets you know he's not the one for this merger. If he responds with the same sentiment about just having a friend and getting to know people, then move forward. Do this quickly and decisively, do not be shy! Beating around the bush because you're afraid of how he may react to your bluntness makes you look weak, and if you want this to work you have to be serious and in control or he'll take you as a joke.

You have a guy in your life that you want to test this on, what do you do practically to lay the foundation? **Call him up, and have phone sex.** Seriously. Call him, and initiate phone sex and see if he's receptive. Phone sex is the ultimate icebreaker;

it drops all formalities and breaks a person down to their nastiest. If you don't know how to have phone sex either you're 16 years old or criminally out of the loop. I assume most reading this know how to phone bone properly, so I won't delve into this step-by-step; email me if you're that stuck and I will be happy to give you a laundry list of filthy conversation starters. After you have phone sex, make the offer. He already knows that you're not looking for a boyfriend yet he's not in the brother role either due to the exchange of "I want you to eat it from the back," dialog. Now it's time to let it be known that you're not looking for a simple, "let's see where it goes" friend, but an adult arrangement that benefits both of you. It doesn't matter the exact wording, so long as you get this point across: *I want someone that I can call up to come handle this without trying to make things more serious than sex, are you up for that kind of arrangement.* 10 out of 10 guys who just jerked off on the phone with you will agree.

How to Test: You made a handshake deal at this point, and as those in business know, some handshake deals aren't worth shit. This professional arrangement is all talk until after you have sex. How will he react after he hits, will you be a good lay, will he be a good layer? I advise having a marathon sex session out the gate. Let him spend the night or make him rent a hotel so you can really get a sense of what he's working with sexually. I'm not talking about dick size, but his ability to please you. There is no excuse for getting into a sexual agreement with a dude who can't make you cum— None! The first time anyone has sex with someone new there are nerves, and while women are going to get wet, men may not get hard, or may not last but a few minutes. Give him an opportunity to make up for the first fuck that same night and give yourself additional time to put it on him just in case you zone out during the first session and revert into a Corpse Bride. By the next morning, you will have decided if he's worth keeping or if his dick game is weaker than a Hulk Hogan leg drop. If he's garbage, don't feel the need to explain your dissatisfaction. When he calls you up, tell him that you're busy. He's not your real friends and you're not his jumpoff, he's your dick, and if you don't want to use him anymore, you don't have to explain shit. After not having time for him or never hitting him up for a rematch, he'll get the hint. Don't be nice! Some women see subpar dick as better than any dick, but you're wasting your time with that guy when you could be out big game hunting for a dude that can make you squirt.

Alternatively, this period is also a good test of his mindset. To be honest, a Spartan pussy will make a man go back on his word, and although you laid the ground rules, he may try to amend them and wife you. If he starts to sweeten up following the sex, his claim about being with the arrangement was just talk, and he's not built to be your convenience cock. Save the drama and cut him off before he grows too attached.

How to Enjoy: You've found a man that can eat and beat like a champ and doesn't try to blur the lines you set, be happy. Don't get lost in the sexual bliss and become too involved. This guy is Papa Johns; you like ordering from him, but he's free to service other people and you're free to order from Pizza Hut...or Rock'n Sushi if you're a little bi-curious. Either way, you have no claim to this man and he has no claim to you, keep that in the front of your mind, because a constant serving of good dick causes female amnesia. Don't ask him who else he's fucking, don't mention other guy's that you may be dating or any other topic that brings to light that you're probably sharing each other. Assume that he's fucking other people, and be okay with that. As long as you're keeping sex safe, it's all good. You can't expect a man to agree to an exclusive fuck buddy; it's not fair nor is it realistic. Even if he tells you that you're the only one he's seeing, he's going to be looking for a woman that can give him what he needs sexually and emotionally. By making it, "you're mine," you turn a relaxed affair into something serious and restrictive. This is supposed to be fun, the second you start thinking about who else he's seeing or if he's lying about seeing other women, you may as well be in a real fucking relationship. You only want sex because you're not ready for the rest, remember that, don't turn the perfect situation into another messy chapter in your life by being sensitive and territorial.

How to Walk Away: I've talked about upgrading relationships in Chapter 19, so I won't get into that aspect or revisit how to remix the rules. Instead, I'll focus on how to walk away from a purely sexual agreement with no hard feelings. There will come a time when he's not acting as into it as he used to be, maybe he's burnt out, maybe he wants more. If this happens, it's time for him to go. You don't need an Allen Iverson dick on your team, aging and going through personal issues that affect his performance. You need a Kevin Durant dick—hungry, willing, and able to put his all into that performance and leave that drama outside the bedroom. Additionally, if you're tiring of sex with him, and it's feeling more like a choir than a rush, cut it off. I know that pussy expires, and I imagine that a penis must go through the same process. You don't owe it to him to keep him on your roster, six weeks or six months in, you always have the option to cancel his contract. Be direct, not cruel, which means tell him straight up that you need a break as opposed to faking an argument that pushes him away. He may try to talk you into coming out of retirement, and you may want to call him up during those first few bored weekends but stand your ground.

Like all good things that come to an end, you have to embrace that it's over and accept that you will have to get out of that comfort zone and look for someone else to scratch that itch. This shouldn't be disheartening; it should be exciting like buying a new car after the lease expires. Why waste this break period with the same fuck buddy for a year? You test drove a dark skin dude with muscles, now go test out a skinny Justin Timberlake looking white boy. Variety is good! Contrary to popular belief, sex is not dirty, it's natural, and if done safely can help relieve stress and anxiety. **Taking a break from love doesn't mean you have to be celibate**. No date zones are to heal. But once you finish healing, or are close to it, there is nothing wrong with having casual sex if that's the kind of woman you are. Some people call this a *Ho Phase*, but it's more like College. Explore yourself! It's more beneficial to explore what you like sexually during a love furlough so there are no questions, reservations, or things left unexplored when you do meet that Game Changer that blows you away and locks you down. Regardless of why you're not looking for a boyfriend now, you will open your heart up eventually, and you will get married. Be able to look back on this time as the chapter where you lived sexually and did the type of nasty shit that would make Ana Steele[1] tap out. You don't have to sit around fingers deep watching Pornhub because you're emotionally unavailable; you can always Spartan up and find a boy toy to get the job done.

The Girl Who Just Wants Companionship

You're good sexually, your spiral dildo and vivid *Muppet Baby* imagination has helped you to master the best vaginal and clitoral orgasms of your life. You don't need a man physically, nor are you the type that has sex without an emotional bond, so a purely sexual relationship is out of the question. However, there remains an emptiness. You want a guy friend to go out with, to talk to, and to spoon with after that *Breaking Bad* marathon...but you know your heart isn't ready to buy into the total package, so breast sucking is about as far as you'll ever let him go. Men hate women like this! Not every boy on girl interaction is either platonic or sexual, it often falls into a semi-platonic box where you admit that you don't want to be bf/gf but concede that you do turn each other on. Nasty joking, flirting, and touching without sex can be seen as a cock tease, but once again, fuck what a man thinks because they invented the art of using women for emotional support. Escapism is common for unhappy men. Sex is teased, but his sole purpose is to lean on a girl who makes him forget about the stress of life until he's ready to open his heart again.

One woman asked why this guy kept calling her every few months, talking about how great she was, yet never initiated anything romantically or even sexually in all the years she had known him. He wanted her companionship, not her box. She was merely a female he could sweet talk and project his feelings on without having to get involved with romantically. This was confusing for her but therapeutic for him. Once a guy like this is over his depression or slump, the phone call or hangout sessions stop, and he goes out to find a real girlfriend. Yes, men do have Rehab Girls who they

---

[1] Anastasia Steele is the female protagonist of the *Fifty Shades of Grey* trilogy

use purely for friendship, and if you are involved with a guy similar to this who talks sex but doesn't press for sex; you are most likely his companion fix. No one ever gives women the green light to use this same method, but I think it's important to learn how to be semi-platonic friends with men that you're attracted to because it serves as a training wheel relationship that can help restore your confidence when dealing with the opposite sex.

I was once involved with a girl who had just gotten out of a four-year relationship and was only two months removed from having an abortion that pretty much ended that love affair. To sum it up, this girl was not ready mentally to have a boyfriend or even a fuck buddy. However, she did need a friend, someone to confide in while her heart healed and help her get to the point where she could trust men again. I didn't sign up for that, and I had no idea all of this had gone on when she first gave me her number to hang out. Despite me wanting something more than just friendship initially, we did become friends. Of course, I tried to have sex, but she guarded that coochie like a goalie and kept it at kissing. I knew there was something holding her back emotionally, so I began to ask her about what had gone on and slowly she revealed her backstory. Instead of running away because I didn't get the sex, I maintained that friendship, still did me, but saved her a seat in my heart because she was a good girl who was fun to hang around. After three months, she began to feel less depressed, and our relationship faded because she no longer needed me to make her feel better. After not speaking for weeks, I received a random booty call. She was ready for sex, and I obliged. We never became an item, and we didn't carry on a physical relationship, it was just sex. She had completed her road back from her breakup and abortion, and this was simple closure.

I share that story to point out that relationships with men, even those that you are attracted to and who are attracted to you, do not have to be sexual. You don't owe a man a blowjob for being your semi-platonic friend, and if you set the rules, you can have his companionship while you take time to heal. Some of you are discouraged because you haven't been able to keep the attention of a man without sex...hell, some of you haven't been able to keep their attention with sex, and so initiating this type of situation is seemingly impossible. Stop having such a low opinion of yourself! A remarkable woman doesn't have to drop her panties or make her mouth work to enchant a man. No matter how much you want to believe, "all guys expect this," or "guys will only put up with this," there are females who men are just happy to have in their lives. Every woman should strive to reach that level of captivation where a man can fall in love with her spirit without the incentive of her vagina. You want to get out of the house and enjoy the company of the opposite sex while you figure your life out then that's exactly what you should do. You can acquire multiple friends who don't get benefits or just one special guy who renews your faith in men, all it takes is initiative.

How to Initiate: Rest assured that the majority of men you spew that, "not looking for anything serious," line to will think you're full of shit. History has shown men that women say that to brace themselves for possible rejection, and rarely does it mean that she doesn't want a boyfriend. You can't convince him verbally that you aren't like the rest of these girls who say that because a girl saying she's different is another thing men hear all the time. You have to prove that you aren't a Relationship Girl with your actions. The ball is in your court, and the only thing you have to do is blatantly define the nature of the relationship during the first week that you're introduced to him. For example, if you exchanged numbers with a guy while waiting at the valet parking stand, call him up and talk to him normally to get a sense of his personality and then hang out with him once before you explain your situation. There is no point in spilling your life story to a guy that may turn out to be a pussy chasing asshole. The same way that I want those women who are strictly looking for dickly to be patient and examine a guy's character, I need you to put that same time in. Women naively fall into the trap that the nice guy they meet that first day or the charismatic guy that's on the other end of the phone the first few days is truly who that man is, but spending time will reveal the truth. If you go out, have a good time, and click with this guy, then make that offer. Inform him that you're taking a break from dating don't go into details, just express how much fun you're having with him and how you'd like to continue it—but only under certain conditions.

Unlike a virgin who shouldn't talk about sex until she gets to know a man for at least a month, you should open up about being celibate and how you're looking for a guy to kick it with...not reverse cowgirl. Be careful how you word this, it's very important not to tease him or lead him on as if he plays his cards right he's going to get some. Avoid the words, "waiting for the right guy," any egotistical male will think he is that right guy and think he just needs to break you down to hit that. Be blunt and tell him that you think he's cool, admit the attraction, but drill into his head that sex is off the table. You want to get to know him, but you don't want to waste his time if he's looking to get some. Once that's understood, give him an out: *If you want to fall back, it's cool but if you're down to just kick it then prove it by calling me this weekend to hangout.* Obviously, a man in your face will tell you what you want to hear, but by passing the ball to him, you see if he's really about this no sex life. Either he'll realize that you're serious and not call you or he'll throw caution to the wind and hit you up to hang, thus agreeing to your rules.

How to Test: Sex will always be the elephant in the room, so talk about it early and often. Not in a teasing way like, "Let me see your dick," but in a joking way like asking nasty questions about things he's done with other women or commenting on other girls you may see on TV or out in public. You don't want to get him hard and horny;

you want to cut through the sexual tension by making it a non-issue so he's comfortable. The second part of this test is to have a house date. Coming over to chill with a guy who knows he's going to get your pussy and you know is going to get your pussy is always a bad idea, but if you are really serious about not wanting sex, just companionship, then you have to put your money where your vagina is. Let him hang in private with you, feel you up (no man is going to sit close to a girl and not get a little feel on, it's virtually impossible), even let him try to go for it. However, by the end of the night, you should have held him off and proven that you aren't a liar.

You may think, "Won't that make him mad and he won't want to hang out anymore," good! If he can't handle being around you with an erection, then he's not going to be able to last long under your rules anyway, this is about weeding out the real from the fake. I had one girl in college who told me, "Feel all the ass you want, but you're just teasing yourself because I ain't taking off these jeans." I was always allowed to touch, but I eventually stopped because as she said, it was only serving to get me all worked up with nowhere to stick. It will take a while for a guy to transition from potential lover to full blown friend, but these first steps test his willpower and yours, and if you can weather the storm, you two may have something special.

How to Enjoy: Take advantage of him by going out to places you want to go. Unlike a boyfriend where you may be afraid to ask him to take you places, this is your boo, he's not taking you anywhere he's simply accompanying you. If money is an issue, you two can go Dutch. If he gets into the habit of trying to pay because he is a gentleman, don't exploit the homie; force him to take your money or surprise treat him. The entire purpose of a relationship like this isn't to use someone financially, but to use him emotionally to help you heal or get your swagger back. We all use someone for something; it's the nature of human beings. Some women use men to make them cum, some use guys to pay their rent, you're using this one to renew your trust in men, and there is nothing shameful in that.

One thing I need to touch on is the guy's other relationships. He's most likely going to be dating other women who he can actually have sex with or dealing with some silly ho that's just giving it up in hopes that she can get the same type of treatment you're getting while keeping your panties on. Do not dwell on his other relationships! Do not make this into "big brother, little sister" and try to get too deep into his love life. If he wants to confide in you for advice, fine, but don't make it a habit to chime in on his girls. This is supposed to be a sanctuary relationship where you two are fake together for those two hours that you hang out. With that in mind, beware of guys who already have girlfriends because the competitive nature of women, even those who don't want anything serious, can leak out and make it a contest for his attention. Keep it light! He's your boy crush you escape from life with, not your boyfriend in training who you have to protect from other women.

How to Walk Away: There may come a point where you begin to want something more, again, I point to Chapter 19 if you're into amending the rules. Most of the time I find that wanting to upgrade this kind of situation is a false alarm; women get comfortable and forget that the goal isn't to fall in love but to fix all of those issues that were holding them back. For instance, if you're still trying to climb that corporate ladder or you're mainly focused on finishing your degree program, you are being hypocritical by trying to turn your companion into your legit boyfriend. Sure, you have time to go out randomly after work or between classes, but this isn't a true relationship where you are expected to spend time. If he were to become your man, please believe that would come with an entirely new commitment and responsibility. If your feelings are getting too invested in a romantic way and you can't turn off that side, then you need to do what my homegirl did and stop calling as much, stop agreeing to hang out as much, and wean yourself off him. Remember he's not meant to be your bff; he's your Rehab Guy. Alternatively, if you see that this dude is really starting to fall in love with you and trying to redefine the rules before you're ready, then you have to be tough and distance yourself.

This distancing can be just as hard as a breakup even though you are technically friends. This isn't a friend zone type guy or someone who you are just cool with; most likely you have that chemistry where if you were in a better space he would be your man. This means that you have to *Old Yeller*[2] his ass. There's no easy way to kill a relationship, you have to face it head on. Confront him in person and say something along the lines of, "You know I love you, but I have so many things that I have to focus on and if we were to make this serious the complications would be a distraction. I can't give you what you want, and I refuse to hold you back, so this has to be it." He'll cry and counter all day long, but you have to follow through and insure that the calls and chill sessions come to a complete stop. Don't end this like a man. Men get into these situations all the time, and after forming a strong non-sexual bond, the female friend often wants to be something more. Yet those guys don't have the balls to let these women off the hook with the truth that he's not ready for that, so the woman becomes depressed, confused, and ends up traumatized from what was supposed to be a relaxed situation. Be better than that, ladies. Keeping a person around who hopes to be with you is selfish. We all know people who are in love can't really go out and find someone new because part of their heart is on hold, desperately waiting for that phone to ring with that person they love on the other end saying they're ready. Don't torture your companion. Even if you aren't completely done healing, even if you don't want to go

---

[2] *Old Yeller* is the tale of a boy and his canine best friend who has to be violently put down. It is the quintessential story of letting go of something you love.

back to being bored, even if you're attached emotionally, it's on you to be the shotgun that puts that dog down.

The Girl Who Just Wants It All

You don't want an on call-penis or a semi-platonic boo thing, you want to date normally with the option to both have sex and lay up under whatever guy you feel like. This section is for you ladies who want a man both as a sexual toy and as a loyal companion...but don't want to get attached. Here's what you do: **Stop lying to yourself**. What I just described isn't having your cake and eating it too, it's having a boyfriend. A guy who comes over to fuck you is just a dick. A guy who comes over just to hang out and talk is a friend. Call it what you want, or don't label it anything, but when you combine sex with quality time you don't get, "Not ready for a relationship," you're in one because that combination creates a fucking boyfriend!

Let's not try to bullshit one another, if you are actively seeking the complete package, yet claiming you're not ready, you are a coward. C-O-W-A-R-D should be the ratchet middle name on your Facebook page because that's what you have become. There are women who honestly aren't ready to date seriously, they have the right to go out, dirty dance on a guy, get his number, and use him as a pastime. Men respect that kind of woman because she's not confusing, she's not trying to Trojan horse her way into his heart, she truly isn't in the right space to love, so she just wants to have fun. Then there are you women who want it all and pretend to be emotionally unavailable, but like tickets to a Tyrese concert you are available, it's just that people aren't lining up to see you.

Bored women who are afraid to date are not the same as damaged women who shouldn't date, but bored women love to front as if they are in that mental struggle. While you talk a good game about having been hurt before or not being ready, the moment you get good dick or you find a shoulder to lean on you start acting weird and asking, "So where's this going..." It's not going anywhere because you said you didn't want a boyfriend. A month and a half later and you're catching an attitude and back to talking about how men are frustrating, but it isn't the man that has stressed you out, you falsified your feelings! It's like those rich kids who started acting like outcasts when Nirvana sparked the grunge movement, lonely ass girls turn into attention whores who want people to think they're only single because they're career driven or unavailable—lies!

I have no stomach for liars and manipulators, especially when there was no reason to lie in the first place, and there are armies of men that feel the same way. You went through a bad breakup, you have a lot of schoolwork, or you work crazy shifts at work, so fucking what! Those women I described at the top of this chapter where the type that truly aren't emotionally ready, you on the other hand are just being lazy and scared. 80% of the women that tell me they don't want to date seriously are full of shit. Real Spartans who come up to me for advice and say, "I'm not looking for the mushy stuff, I just want to get my box ate once a week," they are keeping it real, you on the other hand, are letting your ego and pride mask your true desire for romance. So let's be upfront. You want to start dating again, but you're afraid of one of these three things:

1) HE WILL BE LIKE YOUR LAST BOYFRIEND AND DISAPPOINT YOU.

2) YOU DON'T KNOW HOW TO GET OUT OF THE HOUSE AND ATTRACT THE MEN YOU FIND ATTRACTIVE.

3) YOU ASSUME DECENT MEN RUN AWAY FROM GIRLS WHO EVEN HINT AT WANTING A COMMITMENT DOWN THE LINE.

Admitting you want love is the first step in attracting love. As long as you continue to go about your life pretending you're not looking for something serious, you're going to attract fraudulent men. If you want men to recognize your greatness, start by being honest in terms of what you're looking for. There are females who are grossly overdramatic and cry wolf the moment they have a fallen out with a dude. I know a 19-year-old girl who had maybe two legitimate boyfriends, the last one started playing games, and they broke up. He didn't cheat, beat her, nor did they have a child together that he abandoned. Not to undermine her feelings, but it was a normal breakup. Suddenly she started talking all of this, "I can't give my heart to boys...I need to focus on me...I'll probably never get married because it's messy out here." This is what happens when you sit in front of the computer obsessing over one guy. There was nothing wrong with her, nothing keeping her from getting back out there and interviewing new men, but like a lot of women, this girl followed the leader. The leader being this unified concept of, "Fuck men, all they do is break our hearts." Get over yourself!

You are a girl damn it, and despite what mean mugging ratchets or fake feminist will try to tell you, you do need a man. There is nothing weak about wanting love, and there is nothing foolish about looking for love. Acting like a female is not a negative thing if you are a female! So many modern ladies have been raised or inspired by women who teach this idea that you don't need a man for nothing. Being independent is great, pay your own bills, buy your own car, rah rah rah, but let's get serious; you can't kiss yourself good morning, you can't share inside jokes with yourself, and you can't marry yourself. Girl Power is real, and you don't need males to buy you flowers, kill spiders, or fix your toilet, but don't be so blinded by post modernism that you lie about the emotional need. Men need love, women need love, all humans are fueled by a desire to be loved and appreciated by another person. You can sit there, roll your eyes, and make sidestepping statements like money is the love of your life or your child's unconditional love is enough, but that's not humanly possible. The ultimate feeling that has always driven this species is passionate, romantic love. Admit that you do need a man because even the most prideful man will concede that he needs a woman's love. Take down that ice-cold front and stop hiding your femininity. You don't have to be thirsty for a man or center your life on finding one, but it will save you years of stress and thousands of dollars in therapy if you can freely acknowledge that you want love, but you're afraid that there won't be someone who wants to love you back.

I am certain that every one of you reading this can find a man that will love you the way you desire to be loved. However, if you're hiding behind your school, your job, your child, your weight, your looks, your finances, or your distrust of men then you won't find that life partner, you'll let your prime years slip by and end up settling for Dick. Now let's look at your life one final time. Are you a disciplined woman who needs time to herself to explore life or are you the good girl gone bad chick who needs work on her own issues? If so, go to the top of this chapter and figure out if you want a boy toy, a companion, or time alone. If you are one of these girls who is perfectly capable dating but doesn't want to date seriously because *dating is hard*, then stop perpetrating, and grow the fuck up. There are plenty of quality men to date if you have faith in what you bring to the table. Have the confidence to go out and meet people, have the courage to give men a chance to prove they aren't all the same, and have the emotional maturity to deal with your past trauma until your damage is not only contained but a part of what makes you great.

She Ain't It
Bonus Chapter:

Repairing the Damage
How to Reset a Relationship

fucked up, how do I win him back? I answer this question so much that I have a system of what's worked and hasn't worked over the past several years. Doesn't matter the age of the woman, where she lives, or who the guy is—it's easier than you think to gain forgiveness from a man and start fresh...If you're truly at fault that is. When a man sees a woman as special, he defies this stereotype that women can't earn a second chance. Males know how difficult it is to find that needle in a haystack known as a Game Changer, so no matter how upset he gets or how much time he needs to heal, common sense will point him back to her. Mistakes happen, miscommunication happens, but love can't be denied if the core of that woman proves it wasn't her intent to hurt us. The reason most of your relationships never get another chance is due to your pride and ego. It's easy to say "sorry, babe" but it's difficult for most women with trust issues, Daddy Issues, an affinity for pettiness, and a ton of other insecure traits to go to that man and truly break down why she acted the way she did with transparent accountability. This chapter will help you come clean, not only to earn a second chance but to strengthen yourself moving forward as a Spartan in the making.

Warning: this isn't for those of you desperate to regain something that was never working in the first place. The worst thing to be is a woman chasing after a man that fucked you over, disrespected you, or consistently manipulated you. I don't want any person, man or woman, chasing something unhealthy in the name of heartbreak. **Real isn't what a person says, it's what a person does.**

If the love you want so desperately is just misdiagnosed obsession, then you need to let go, not look to fix the unfixable. Don't take this advice and use it on a piece of shit man just because you hate rejection! These steps are for very specific people, those that deserve a second chance because they now realize the error of their ways and are looking to improve. If you feel it isn't your fault, want a quick fix because you hate to be alone, or are still blind to the parts of you that are damaged then don't waste your time reading this chapter. You will get back only to break up again. This chapter is for women specifically, as I want the men who have made it through this entire book and now understand what it takes to be a King worthy of a Queen, to be able to share this with someone they see potential in before agreeing to give that relationship another chance. Consider it couples therapy in book form.

Pre-Condition Yourself for Change

How do you become a great girlfriend if you have never been in a real relationship or a healthy relationship? There isn't a blueprint on how much attention, care, or space you should give someone so they feel that you're truly down for them. Relationships are like Kool-Aid, it takes several tries before you know the amount of sugar x water x flavoring that hits that perfect sweet spot. Every man is different, so the shit that Anthony needed, Ray may not. The direct and blunt way you give your opinion was what Steven needed, but it turns Jason off. Get the picture? Dating someone isn't just about exposing their motives it's also about learning how their personality meshes or doesn't mesh with your own. For those of you that have only had bad relationships, it's even harder to understand that you don't need to be so hard or bitchy, and that not every man is like your fuckboy ex. I remember dating a girl that was all jacked up in the head due to the things her last boyfriend put her through. It got to the point where it went from being attractive in a Nomi from *Showgirls* way to unbearable. To this day that girl is still unmarried, and it's because she fell into the trap of treating all men as if they were the enemy.

Reflect on how you think you are versus how you actually act when in a relationship and that will point you to how much work you need to do before you try to get back with someone. You can't receive someone great if you don't know how to be great your damn self. The first step in getting beyond any of the issues listed in this chapter is to own them. No more of this "I don't know why..." bullshit. You do know why a man stops reaching out as much, breaks up, or simply disappears. The truth is you don't want to admit the reason things fell apart or are falling apart because you know you must accept most of the guilt, and for women that are used to being defensive or in the right, this is a hard pill to swallow. Let go and be honest. This starts with looking back at the friction. **When was the first time you argued? When was the first time you felt him act differently? When was the first time you raised your voice, or he raised his voice?** Nothing happens out of the blue, and if you swear it does, then that means you don't pay attention to details. I know people personally that are so up their own ass and so self-absorbed that they can't see when they piss people off or when someone is agitated. I want you to take yourself through your relationship, and if you can't go "Ah-ha" a few times, then you are exactly the type of person I just described. Before you move forward, jot down those instances where you felt things had changed in the dynamic of your relationship. It could be something as simple as this:

Date & Action: Week 4. He didn't call back when he usually is good about that.

Possible Reason: We talked earlier, and he didn't sound himself, so I told him to call me back when he felt like talking. Maybe the way I said that could have sounded like I was annoyed with him because I was annoyed that he was just breathing on the phone and not engaging.

Write each instance down in that way with as many details as you can point to, real or imagined, because as you list each situation, you'll begin to connect the dots. Most people can't do that because it's about ME ME ME. If you say, "Well he gave me attitude or disinterest, so I gave it right back," you're being defensive. No one wins because no one cuts through the misunderstanding. Sometimes it's the way you say something, text something, or refuse to inquire about someone's mindset that lays the groundwork for the relationship falling apart. For instance, I had a girl ask me about a situation with her boyfriend. She took a picture of her new hairstyle and sent it to him. He replied that it was blurry. She responded back, "Well I posted it on Instagram." He never wrote back or liked the picture on Instagram even though he actively liked other pictures. This caused a rift, and she didn't know what his problem was. I pointed out when someone asks about a picture, and your response is to look at it elsewhere that sounds like you're being a smartass. As a boyfriend, that feels as if you're saying, "Go look with the rest of the peasants." Even though she didn't mean it that way, you can't tell in a text what the tone or subtle meaning may be. These are the things I want you to pull out of yourself right now as you write the <u>Date</u>, <u>Action</u>, and <u>Possible Reason</u> for any and every moment of friction in your relationship. Once you have your list, you will be able to go through the qualities below, see which fits your situation, and utilize the resolution.

The Girl That Was Too Smothering & Attention Starved

Problem: There's no bigger proof that people don't pay attention to one another's personality traits than a relationship that feels like a cage. You want to spend all your free time with your boyfriend. You hate when he goes out with his friends. You can't go a full day without checking in several times. You make plans for the both of you without consulting with him first. You stop by unannounced or expect him to come over to see you the moment he's off work or out of class. Every day is supposed to be like Lady and the fucking Tramp because you think a relationship is about being up each other's ass 24-7.

Women love two things—attention and their birthdays. The idea of "in love" for those who have never truly been in love puts this pressure on a woman to expect constant showering of love and affection to feel secure. You ever see two teenagers in the mall? Holding hands, grinning, and everything is "babe this...babe that," that shit isn't love! Love is a silent engine that powers a strong relationship, not the over exaggerated cuteness of the honeymoon stage when your hormones are at a 10 and you can't stop smiling at one another. **For love to settle in, lust has to fade.**

Lust is a false high, an emotional narcotic that rewires your brain and makes you feel euphoric for a time. Most people stop talking within three months because it was all lust. Love keeps that fire going, but it's not raging like in a movie. A man who wants to start building with you needs to make you a part of his real life, not a vacation powered by lust. By real life I mean that he's going to do other things for fun, he's going to be stressed and need time to think alone, he's going to want to get immersed in work and career building and not be in the right mindset to always hang out with you. He has to be positive that the moment he's doing him, you aren't going to take that as a sign that he's cheating or growing bored. To be there when he needs you and secure enough not to get mad when he doesn't want to be bothered, is how you fit into a man's life and prove that it could last forever. A woman that understands how to love when close by and from a distance is truly special. Those ladies that want that teenage crush love can't fit into a man's life because they will always want to be the center. The insecurity of not feeling loved unless he's in her face proves that she will always be a hindrance. What happens when you cling to man or always thirst for his attention?

Result: Men need the freedom to roam and live life. Even those guys that start off being just as clingy as you were during the honeymoon stage will eventually settle in. Lust gives way to normalcy, and once that happens he will still want to see you, but it won't be every day or every weekend. **Absence makes the heart grow fonder, but being attached at the hip makes the resent build faster.** First, it'll start with him making an excuse as to why he's too busy to see you. Then it'll be placing the blame on others. He wants to see you, but he has to do something for his mother or his brother. These are white lies he's utilizing because he's burnt out already but doesn't want to make it into an argument. To tell a woman, "I need a day to myself," will create an attitude. Even those of you that say, "I like my time too," are the first ones to internalize a man not wanting to answer your phone call or hang out as a form of rejection. You pretend that it's cool, then your mind goes into overdrive—*why does he want time to himself suddenly, is it someone else?* Yes, a man should communicate his feelings, but when he wants to make it work, he puts up with your behavior in silence because it's not yet a deal breaker or worth fighting over.

The breakup or distancing comes once the smothering turns into suffocating. For example, you pick up on the fact that he's growing distant and it sparks an argument that he's been waiting for. Without warning, he throws your actions in your face. You may not even know you've been smothering until he comes with receipts that put you on the defense. Here you were thinking you were a good girlfriend, and there he is telling you how much you annoy him. That shit hurts, and you both say things you may not mean, which leads to a rift. Alternatively, it can be more silent. He starts being way too busy to the point of avoidance and you read the writing on the wall, and you both agree to go on break without things being addressed.

Resolution: Get off this prideful notion that it's his fault for not being honest about how he was feeling in the relationship. We established that he should have communicated, but the problem remains that you are a smothering ass human being that didn't know how to pull back. It's your actions, not his lack of telling you about your actions that is the issue—accept that. No one should have to tell you how to be normal. Yes, a man should try and teach his woman the things she doesn't know, but I've witnessed women lashing out the moment you try to help them. No woman wants to be checked, so here's where you check yourself. Let things cool off for a week or two. Do not be so upset or overcome by depression that you try to force a conversation before you both have had time to reflect. **The top problem a woman has post-breakup is impatience**. It's broken, and you want to fix it the next day because your heart hurts like a motherfucker—deal with it! Fall back and chill out. Think about things from his POV, so when you do talk you can ask questions to understand the larger issue, not to defend your actions as if you're in the right. When you do reach out, set up a phone call where you talk or someplace public where you can meet. Don't back yourself into a text battle. You can't communicate properly through blocks of text! Don't go over his place or have him come by yours because sex will most likely happen. You can't move forward if you put the band-aid of make up sex on right away.

Have a conversation where you ask him how he felt during the relationship and to name specific ways you weren't a good partner. In this case, it's smothering, so he will try to spare your feelings to an extent because it's not that a man doesn't want to spend time with his girlfriend, he just needs individual space as well, and it's hard to communicate that idea without a girl being offended. **"So, your friends make you happier than me," is a common clap back, and proves that some women just don't understand the concept of space.** If you feel him dodging the question or being abstract, point out the obvious. Again, take a few weeks to wrap your head around everything that's gone down because you'll have to bring up things you did to see what exactly bothered him. "Was wanting you to come over after work all the time a bit too much," is one example of opening a conversation up to talk about real things that you can change moving forward. The first conversation shouldn't be a, "let's get back together" conversation. You need to restart slow. If you talk the first time on the phone, the second time meet up in person and talk some more.

The final step will be to swallow that pride and tell him what you're willing to do to get back together. I know a lot of you don't like asking or begging as it makes you feel weak and vulnerable, but this is where parts of the *Ho Tactics* psychology works every time. A man doesn't like to tell a woman he likes/loves "no" or turn his back on her unless she's done something horrible. To come with your hat in hand and tell him you're willing to work on specific things you did, not just this bullshit general notion of doing better than before, will open his soft side up to giving you another chance. Furthermore, tell him that he has every right to point out your behavior if you're doing it again. This is not to give him power over you, it's to learn your blind spots via another person. You all do things you don't realize you're doing unless it's brought to your attention. Even if this relationship fails again for other reasons, knowing exactly how you can be at your worst will help you catch yourself in your next relationship before it becomes an issue.

The Girl That Was Always Accusing & Wouldn't Leave the Past Behind

Problem: Men fuck up...a lot. If you're going to forgive him, you don't have to forget, but you can't move forward thinking you have a right to throw that past incident or incidents in his face. I often advise women that if the trust is destroyed that they should move on because the average woman will always have a short memory when it comes to betrayal and she will go there if a situation reminds her of that past indiscretion. If you didn't heed this advice or thought it was something you could get beyond then you must be a woman of your word. You argue, and it's, "Who are you to judge me when you did XYZ..." You suspect he's up to something and you go snooping through his things and justify it with, "I know how you are." You invade his privacy, call his friends to make sure he is where he said he was, or stalk him to be sure he's not playing you. Every girl at work is his "girlfriend." Every girl he follows on social media is "the bitch you really want." How long do you think a man can put up with that before he looks for an exit?

Result: A man can only take so many lashes before he figures out he's being emotionally blackmailed and you aren't ever going to let the past go. Saying "sorry" isn't always enough, but when you agree that it was enough then turn around and remind him that the apology meant nothing, how can he ever prove himself again? I've heard several men tell me, "If she's accusing me of it, I may as well do it." You're going to be angry regardless if he did fall asleep at his cousin's place overnight or if he was laid up with another bitch, so he may as well get the reward of smashing new pussy. Other men have the mentality that they would rather be alone than constantly argue over things that he hasn't done. Either way, if you push him into the arms of someone else or push him to break up with you for his sanity, you can't be upset with him, your inability to stay true to your word caused it.

Resolution: You must commit to real improvement in the form of forgiveness. I had a woman I was advising set up weekly therapy sessions where she could talk about where her hurt was coming from. In her case, she had a boyfriend that was Facebook messaging some girl sexual things and in her mind unless she could have access to his passwords she couldn't move on. He gave his passwords to her as a sign of his good faith, but that wasn't good enough as she still found ways to a fight. I suggested that she open up to him about her therapy by writing an email each week about what was talked about and what she learned about dealing with her issues. By the fourth week of her therapy and only two weeks of sending these emails, he wanted to meet with her and give it a second chance so long as she stayed in therapy. Those two are now engaged.

"Let's work on it," requires real work, not just sweeping it under the rug and pretending it didn't happen. He has to work on never doing what he did again, and you have to work on not letting your imagination run wild while he's trying to regain your trust. To win your man back, you need to prove that you are evolving from that accuser mindset. It's not enough to say, "I won't bring it up again," because most likely you said that before and it happened without you being able to control it. To counteract flying off the handle or giving into basic emotions, you must seek real help in coming to grips. Friends, therapy, reading books, keeping a journal, these are all steps in the right direction while you heal. In the meantime, be a man's friend again. Let him in on how you're trying to change. Once you establish a real friendship that's not about getting back together, having sex for old time's sake or any selfish reason, a man will take you back without you even asking because that rage and fear about repeating the past will have faded by then. **A guy who hurt you feels guilty, remember**

that. The reason you're acting this way is due to his initial action, right? Therefore, to see that you're trying to get over this and that you need a partner to help you heal the damage he caused, will appeal to any man with true feeling for you.

The Girl That Thinks She's Mommy

Problem: There's a difference between a woman that has the qualities of your mother and one that thinks she is your mother. Men can be big babies, they often act helpless and needy, which leads a lot of women with unrealized maternal issues slipping into that role of taking care of a man like he's her big kid. That's all cute and innocent at a certain level, but it can quickly lead to being overbearing. Telling a man, not asking him. Trying to solve all his problems for him. Catching an attitude when he doesn't take your advice. Throwing "I told you so," if something he did didn't work out. A man asking you to help with his resume doesn't mean you go the extra mile and try to find him a job. A man asking you for your advice doesn't mean he should follow it to a Tee. A man asking you for financial help doesn't give you the right to throw that back in his face or hold it over his head if he's not making the moves you want him to make with that money. Guys swallow pride to ask for help or to let you in on worries. For you to take over as if you know what's best, emasculates him. You feel that you're a partner, but you're not, you're being Mommy #2, and no man wants to live the rest of his life being told what he should or shouldn't do.

Result: The first thing to go will be communication. A guy who feels he's being reigned over will keep things to himself. This starts with the small things then leads to the big things. You'll begin to realize that those nice conversations you used to have at night have been replaced by watching movies in silence or him giving you short responses when you ask about his day. I have a friend that was engaged, and he realized after the proposal his girl's attitude began to change. She felt entitled to tell him how to live life as if being his soon to be wife meant exercising more control. He got wrote up at work, and came home to vent to her about his manager and how he wasn't at fault. Instead of taking his side, or better yet, simply listening to him let that frustration out. She reminded him that he couldn't afford to get fired with the wedding coming up and told him he needed to apologize to get it removed from his record. He didn't do that. When he ended up being fired a few months later for arguing with that manager, she took it upon herself to go up and try to get his job back. This drove a wedge between them where he decided not to vent to her again. By the time they selected a wedding venue he had told me they were barely speaking because he couldn't say anything without her two cents being thrown in his face as if he didn't know shit and she had all the answers. I told him that it's pointless to get married to a woman you can't even talk to because you're afraid of her reaction. Sure, enough he called the wedding off, and she claimed not to know where they went wrong. In her book, she was the perfect woman, he was just ungrateful.

Men shut down emotionally more often than it rains in Seattle. Males aren't internal beings by nature, but they learn to be introverted around women whom they feel don't allow their voice to be heard. You may think he's dramatic or having some form of male PMS, but the reality is if a man goes from being your best friend to barely sharing the details of his life, he no longer sees you as a partner. Guys will stay with these women for extremely long times because the love is still there and the wife type things they do are appreciated, but dudes like this are high chances for cheating because emotionally their needs aren't being met.

Resolution: You can't control other people's lives. You can try, you may even bully some into allowing it, but no lasting relationship is built to be a one-way street. You must address your behavior in a real way before you approach him in hopes of forgiveness and understanding. Why do you want to tell a man what to do? Because you don't trust his judgment. Maybe for a good reason, but the way to improve someone's flaws isn't to take over, it's to work with them to help see those flaws in the first place. When a mother teaches her son to ride a bike she doesn't push him off and ride it herself; she has to work patiently to reinforce the lesson without being a nuisance. If your boyfriend shuts down on you, help him open up by being direct about the problem you see forming. Don't catch an attitude and give him the silent treatment, don't curse him out about being secretive, address the elephant in the room. "I think you don't talk to me about certain things because of how I tend to react, is that true?" Again, men don't want to get into a fight so have receipts ready for when he says, "I don't know what you're talking about, we talk all the time." This isn't a fight; it's a confession: *It's okay, I'm admitting that I don't always listen without having to chime in and that I try to tell you what to do. I want to work on that, so you feel comfortable telling me anything.* If you love a man, then you have to go to that place where most women hate going and take self-inventory.

This idea of it's on both of you isn't always true. I repeat, an issue that's related to your behavior can't be dismissed by pointing fingers at him for not speaking on it. If he's being quiet, it's proof that he wants to avoid confrontation and save what you have. That's foolish on his part because a problem unmentioned will fester until it erupts. Own you overbearing nature, have examples of the things you're sorry for doing and a man will begin to open back up and heal what's been damaged because every man wants his woman to be his best friend.

The Girl That Put Everyone
in Your Business:

Problem: We live in a world where the internet has become the new dairy. No matter if she's introverted or extroverted, going online and posting about something that's happening is not only empowering it's therapeutic. However, in a relationship, things happen from day-to-day where you go from extreme highs to extreme lows, and they don't need to be broadcast while you're upset. Your boyfriend pisses you off by standing you up on date night because he says he fell asleep. In that moment, you can't stand him, so you blast off a Facebook post or a Snap about people being full of shit—and by people, everyone knows you mean your boyfriend. You have a bad argument where you both say things you will want to take back the next day, but in the hour after that fight, you're still fired up, so you unleash that fury. If it's not the internet, then you call your best friend, cousin, mother, platonic male "friend" that secretly wants to fuck you, or anyone that will listen and you lay out all the ways your boyfriend is a piece of shit. Of course, the next day you erase that Facebook post, re-friend him, and tell your confidant that you were just in your feelings and everything is good. The problem is that it's not good. The worst thing you can do is betray the confidentiality of a relationship by telling the world. When you're a teenager, it's expected, but as an adult to not be able to handle your anger to the point where you have to unload the bitch clip online or run down your personal details to a friend makes a man think twice about how long you can last.

Result: A man's reputation is right up there next to his dick in terms of things he takes pride in. No man wants strangers judging him on half a story told in the heat of a moment by an emotional nut job. Nor does a man want to have friends and family hearing with full bias all the ways he isn't a good boyfriend. It's not about other people's opinions; it's about having to go and live life in that mess that a girl made. Imagine being a man that must go over to a girl's mother's house two weeks after she told her about you shaking her, tossing her clothes out of the closet, and wrestling the house key away. The mother doesn't care that you two are fine now nor wants to hear your side, she now sees you as a monster. Imagine being a man that has to log onto Facebook after his girl tells her timeline that you're a small dick, no money having, liar. People can't un-see that, and everyone from your close friend to your work associates are now looking at you differently. All the "baby I'm sorry, you know how I get," followed by a sloppy blowjob can't change the fact that a girl like that will most likely repeat that cry for help action every time you have a fight.

Resolution: The same way you got yourself into this mess, you get yourself out. If you're big and bold enough to air someone out online and defame their name, be woman enough now to post a follow-up publicly apologizing for what you did. This isn't just to appease him, as that won't take back what you said, but it makes that "I'll never do it again," mean something going forward. For you to expose your quick temper and petty response to drama for all to see, ensures that if you do it again, those same people will now remember back to that apology and take what you're currently saying with a big-ass grain of salt. Furthermore, if the problem is telling other people how horrible he is, own up to them about your issues so they can give you advice, not just be someone who will listen to you bash someone you're just going to get back with at the end of the week. People love messy bitches because they have all the fun stories. Everyone from your mom to that girl you think is your BFF, will bring you up in conversation and tell the world, "I don't know why she doesn't leave him," because in their book you're a dummy for staying with a jerk. **Talk about your problems, don't just talk about the person**.

Lastly, you must let your boyfriend in on why you can't contain yourself, then offer up a solution. The best things that have worked for women I advise is to do a cooling off period of 24 hours without contacting anyone. No social media, no texting, no calling. Write out your thoughts in a personal diary. Talk aloud about how mad you are. Go through the motions of your feelings, but always sleep on it before you take actions. Showing a man that you're not only sorry but you now have a way to prevent that will open him up to testing that, and that's all you need, a chance to prove you won't repeat that mistake and that he can trust you.

The Girl That Keeps Breaking Up

Problem: Every time you and your boyfriend go through a rough patch your solution is to run away. You would rather quit than talk it out, forgive, or work towards a compromise because you are deathly afraid that this is proof that he's not the right one. There are women with extreme fear of failure in terms of relationships. The concept of wasting time with someone that didn't want you has existed long before SZA was even born. The reality that I've covered in exhaustion on my website is that most men only see you as a Placeholder, a woman filling a seat until he finds something better. I talk about this to help you see the red flags not to turn you paranoid. However, some women are like hypochondriacs. They see small problems or normal arguments as that proof that he's no good. If you break up with every man that does something that can be worked out, you never develop the skills you will need for a deeper relationship, let alone years of marriage where rough patches will pop up in waves. By running away, you're making yourself into a hurdler that refuses to practice with hurdles then wonders why they keep stumbling when they have to race for real. You need to train yourself how to overcome relationship obstacles!

I talk to a lot of serial breakup artist. These types use breaking up as an ultimatum to make a man act right. Men do get in check when a woman they truly love breaks up because they know how unique she is even with this flaw. Even those guys that play tough will crawl back with an "I miss us," text if you break up. These types of women know this for a fact, hence using it as a ploy as opposed to being sincere. The fucked up thing is that when you do that every few months, you start to decay his love for you. I've never seen an adult relationship that was on and off last or led to a marriage that didn't end in divorce—never. You're killing someone's fear of losing you when you play the breakup card, and you're also dwindling their love with each new, "I think we should take a break," scare tactic.

Result: Eventually that "I miss you text," won't come again. Eventually meeting up to have sex won't bring you two back together. Eventually your man will find someone else while you're in the midst of pushing and pulling and she will be a better fit for him than you ever allowed yourself to be. You could have been his Game Changer, but you devolved yourself into a Placeholder because you run from confrontation instead of addressing it. It's okay not to talk to your boyfriend for a few days or a week while you cool off. Breaking up should be the final solution when things can't be cooled off, talked about, or resolved with both sides in agreement of what needs to change. Breaking up as a manipulation tool will always leave you single and bitter. Your excuse is that he did all of these things that led to the breakup, and someone else will point out how you never worked on any of those qualms, you just ran and came back as if "sorry" is the same as discussing what you needed to see. Since you didn't learn the lesson of how to communicate and put in real effort, the next guy you meet will get a woman that still handles shit like a 16-year-old. The cycle of these start-and-go relationships every six months will continue for life or until you get desperate enough to settle for someone you don't want.

Resolution: Stay in the fucking saddle! Understand the issue that's pushing you apart and talk to him about it without getting into a shouting match. If he's not doing something you expect a boyfriend to do like plan proper date nights, give consistent attention, or stop hanging out with girls you don't approve of, tell him that in exact words, not in a "do this or else" way.

How a brat handles her wants: *If you really loved me you would take me out on more dates. I need someone that values me and wants to do more than eat pizza and stay in. It's over!*

How a woman handles her wants: *I know you're tired after work, but I feel we need to have a date night once a week because I'm not feeling the affection, what do you think?*

From there you both discuss that issue. He may have excuses, but it doesn't matter, you're being an adult and presenting what you want and if he does love you, he will adjust to that. It's better to explain how you're feeling, not be a brat that cries about not getting something and threatens to take her pussy and go home. A man understanding you without threats is how you grow together, a man who just does things to shut you up or because he's afraid you'll leave, will eventually grow distant. No one is a mind-reader, sometimes relationships get so comfortable that men take women for granted, don't get mad, let it be known via a conversation, not an ultimatum.

The Girl That Lied & Cheated

Problem: Women are masters of keeping secrets. I'm privy to some mind-blowing stories that I haven't shared with anyone, especially males because I know it would raise the question, "are all women like that?" When it comes to relationship ruining lies, most women will safeguard that secret while others will confess for fear that it will eat them alive if held in. You lied and said you went to a friend's house, but you met up with your ex for closure. You lied and said you needed emergency money, but you just wanted to go shopping. You gave your phone number out to a guy, but you lied and said your girlfriend gave it out and you had no idea. These are just a few instances where you misled your boyfriend then he found out about them either from you or through evidence that you're full of shit, and now you have to either think of another lie or come clean. On the other hand, is the issue of cheating. Most women I've talked to fall into the following: Cheating because he's never around to give her emotional reassurance. Cheating because an ex came back in her life. Cheating because she still hasn't forgiven his cheating. Cheating because she's not being satisfied sexually. What happens when a man finds out that you're a liar, a cheater, or both?

Result: Getting over a woman cheating is harder than a day-old ass injection. Women complain that guys get 3rd and 4th chances after they put their dicks in something else, but women are shown the curve if she even sexts another guy. This is mostly true because a man internalizes cheating in a competitive "my property" way that's nearly impossible to get over. Women often look at the looks of the other woman her man cheated with to shed light. A man doesn't care about how another man looks when cheating happens; he's more insulted that this other guy did something he couldn't or had something more appealing. Think of the things men are most jealous of—money and power. To quote Chris Brown, "Just got rich, took a broke nigga's bitch..." That lyric cuts to the heart of male insecurity. The majority of men that I know have slept with another guy's girl at least once. I used to get off on it because it is an ego stroke for this girl to say she loves someone else then come running when you call. That's what I mean by competitive. You let another man get your number—why? You let another man charm your panties off—why? You let another man suck on you and penetrate you—why? At each step, you were saying via those actions that he had something you wanted more than your boyfriend and that wounds the male ego to the point where he may not be able to come back to you or even love another woman for a very long time.

Regarding telling lies, a man will automatically jump to, "What else is she capable of doing," because a person that lies once will lie again unless they truly feel remorse. I had an ex-girlfriend who would always lie to her mother and friends. I would be next to her while she was on the phone and think, "she doesn't even need to lie about that," but she was addicted to it. She cheated on me, then years later when she was in a relationship, she cheated on her new guy with me. Her personality was that of a habitual liar because she never saw the harm. A man will most likely forgive you for lying, but that trust will bend to the point where he's not going to invest his all in you again until you've shown some consistency in the way you live, not just around him but around everyone.

Resolution: Are you sorry you did it or are you sorry you got caught? You have to be 100% honest before you try to heal this rift. If there's something in you that lies just to lie or cheated because you just wanted something new and exciting, then you will do it again when tempted. I always reference the Julia Roberts movie *Closer* when I talk about cheating because it's the closest thing to reality I've ever seen regarding what a man needs to move forward, not with the woman, but with himself. A guy wants details because through details he finds understanding, and through understanding, he can make peace. **Therefore, don't fucking lie about your reasons.** If you gave a guy your number, own that shit. You thought he was cute and it was a night where you needed to feel attractive. This opens up a conversation where you both can talk about why you don't feel pretty and what he's done to make you feel you need validation from another man. My friend is bisexual, and she fell in love with a woman that said she was a Registered Nurse. My friend found tax records on her computer that listed her occupation as an LPN, not an RN and the corresponding salary. It was a small thing to lie about, and my friend was ready to forgive her, but she held on to the lie. When she couldn't lie her way out of it, she caught an attitude and told her she shouldn't have been snooping. That relationship ended not on the lie, but the woman's inability to give understanding to the lie. Walk them through your reasons no matter how painful or how deep it exposes your negative qualities. A person that loves you wants to forgive you but they need to see that this isn't a reflection of your true character, just a reflection of something you mistakenly felt you had to do.

Regarding cheating, I see two directions. The first is when he breaks up. The second is when a man stays with the woman and claims he can get past it but he struggles. If you're currently in this situation, you most likely notice that things remain tense and he still hasn't transitioned into his normal self. This means it's constantly on his mind even when he doesn't want it to be. If the scar isn't healing, then you must open the bandage and find out why. Most likely you two didn't discuss what happened in real terms. "I don't know why it happened. I was stupid!" Yeah right. **Stupidity, alcohol, your friends, or drugs aren't excuses for cheating they're just cover-ups.**

Women normally cheat for emotional reasons as opposed to purely physical ones, so talk about the way you felt in the weeks or months before it happened. This doesn't always point to something your boyfriend did wrong, it may reveal something you were hiding internally. A woman that's afraid that she's falling too hard could try to self-sabotage by using sex to push away a man whom she feels is too good for her. A woman that feels as if she's losing control in a relationship or her identity is being swallowed could lean on sex as a way to show that she is in charge and can still do as she pleases. Even if he is at fault, don't feel you're adding insult to injury because he must know what went wrong if this is going to work again. Be brutally honest! If a man thinks this was just an anomaly or random circumstance, how will he know you'll never cheat again? A woman that cheats with no true motive is a scary individual because he can't ever say that he knows her, because that reasoning means that if the wind blows she may get horny. You know why you did it, confess. Talk about it in detail, cry, apologize, and if things haven't changed talk about it again. Open communication must be reestablished, and a deep understanding has to be cemented for him to take you back. Men are the most tempted people in the world, so trust that he will show empathy so long as you show honesty.

There are numerous hiccups when it comes to love that goes beyond these examples, but no matter if your problem is listed or isn't, the fact remains that the first step will always be to label what you're doing that's turning someone off and driving them away. If you can't name it, you can't dissect it. Saying generalized bullshit like, "I know I have an attitude," or "I have trouble trusting people," won't tell you shit about what you do that is hurting your relationship nor how to fix it. Your actions should be broken down first, then you can connect the dots back to things like trust issues, your parents, being picked on when you were little, feeling as if you need to compete with others, and the list goes on. Every action you take is reacting to something going on consciously or subconsciously, and if you're hurting the people you love or downgrading your character, the thing you're reacting to has to be sniffed out. It's hard to go inside and talk about how you live above your means because you grew up with a friend that always made you feel poor and inferior. It's hard to admit that you lust for casual sex as a way to take back control from this idea that no man, even your father, ever wanted you on a real level. And it's extremely hard to look at a failing relationship and admit that it's more on you than him because you're walking around with a litany of issues you don't want to address and an ego that needs to believe that you're not typical or damaged. To become a Spartan, to live in honesty and awaken your True Self, means you have to rip away all the false notions of how great you are when the results aren't adding up.

If you were a Game Changer, the game would be changing. If you're stuck repeating mistakes and losing at love, then that's proof of internal problems. If every relationship you're in ends negatively or if you're unable to list a reason other than the other person being toxic time and time again, then you're doing yourself a disservice. The common denominator in your relationships is YOU. Some men won't be a good fit, and some relationships are meant to end. Nevertheless, you can't be so defensive and stuck in your ways that you avoid the possibility that you need work, healing, and analysis to grow into the woman whom you know you can be but haven't quite become. Don't miss out on the love Your Universe is trying to offer to you by refusing to evolve. Know your strengths... Know your weaknesses... Know that if it's real love, a man will always forgive you because there isn't a woman alive that will ever be a greater match for him than you.

He Will Never
See You as Special

*N*o matter what I write to empower and put control in the hands of womankind, one big stumbling block will be the male point of view. Lovesick women don't care about why men act the way they act nor are they interested in the psychology of users and abusers, they just want to know what they're doing wrong and how to quickly get a man to change his mind to see them as special. Look at the titles of dating advice books: *How to Text a Guy. How to Pray with a Guy. The Power of Being Submissive. The Power of Being a Bitch.* **They're trying to transform you into what you're not. I'm trying to destroy the weak parts of your character to restore you to what you truly are!** See the difference? I won't lie to you. Supreme confidence, having value, being no-nonsense, that won't guarantee that the guy you're crushing on comes over and asks for your number or that the guy you're in a relationship marries you. It's meant to supercharge you so that you can swing for the fences and not feel rejected when it doesn't work out. It's meant to pull you up so that you can make demands in a current relationship and be okay walking away if your man doesn't want to give you what you deserve. What I write about gives you the upper hand, it ensures that you will always be able to find a new candidate and that no man will ever waste your time because you know the signs. Nevertheless, most of you could give two fucks about "girl power" you want the type of guys you want to see you as a Unicorn.

The hard truth is that every man has a personal want that you will either meet or fail to meet. You're thinking about yourself. Stop. Think about this from the perspective of a male. Point to his entire life, it will show you what he's after and what he loathes. Do you realize that how a man's mother treated him can keep you from ever being his wife? Do you know that his first girlfriend cheating on him could keep him sabotaging a good thing? Do you understand that something as simple as how his

Dad or uncles talked about women could have poisoned him for life? **You can't force a man to be right for you just because you love him.** You can't fix a broken man. You can't charm a man who isn't into your type. Being a Spartan is about power, not some delusion that every man you want to be right for you can shed their personal preferences, biases, or trauma to be right for you.

The solution to your stress isn't to keep racking your brain on how to make yourself special in the eyes of some guy, it's to understand what turns a man on and what turns him off based on his personality type and life experiences. Let's start by clearing up the bullshit Basica propaganda that's still rattling around in your head. This idea that "if a man chases you that means he wants you," is a myth. A male's lust for your pussy has nothing to do with you as a person. Men don't see personality at first, we see a vagina. Men only stop seeing you as vagina, when you clearly demonstrate that he can't get away with the same bullshit that typical girls let him get away with.

Most women say they're different but rarely show their difference. You don't challenge men, you roll over. You don't want to risk pushing him away with questions that gage his motives or tests that prove whether he's been paying attention during those conversations or just nodding along. Women compromise their value to earn "she's cool" approval. By being low-maintenance and like "one of the boys" you think he'll see you as a catch. False. If you try to fit in like his exes, he'll see you in the same light as those women. If you try to mother him and baby him into loving you, he'll see you as subservient, and that could remind him of the mother, aunt, or family member that got played like a dummy. Each man has baggage. **When you try to pretend to be something you're not just to kiss his ass, you're most likely feeding into a reason to hate you.** All the time you spend texting and talking to these guys, you haven't figured out that they PMS more than women? Incompatible men stick out like a sore thumb because they will greet your kindness with huffing and puffing. You think his inconsistencies are due to something you're lacking. In actuality, they're a product of his own demons. These are easy red flags to spot, but you're not trying to figure him out, you're trying to fit into his life, so he continues to like you. That's why you try to change for a man, read books that tell you what to do, and why you play yourself to keep a man who isn't compatible.

I was once asked, "Why do men say they want certain things, get it, then leave for someone who doesn't do those things." If a money hungry person loses their wallet, and someone says they'll replace what was stolen, that person won't say the wallet was empty. **They make up a high but believable amount and cash in on that kindness.** If a girl asks a man what he wants in a woman, he's going to say one that doesn't go out much, covers her body, is loyal to a fault, sucks his dick like a champ, doesn't nag, gives him space and privacy... **they make up fantasy wifey traits and cash in on a naïve woman's want to impress him.** Every time you ask that dumb ass question of "*What are you looking for*," you're setting yourself up to get robbed! A man doesn't want a slave that buys into his fantasy, he wants a fucking Queen that says, "*fuck what you want, this is who I am*!" A woman should never set out to become what one particular man claims he's looking for, her only goal is to become so secure in her value that she doesn't give a fuck what these men want if it isn't her. That sense of worth will make you intuitively what all men of value are looking for—His Match.

Before a man can see you as his match, however, he must first have respect for you. This is a misogynistic world, that's not going to change. It's the way the game board of life is set up, and while there are nice men who open doors for you and march for women's rights, you will never know the full of extent of what males really say about females behind closed doors. I do because we men are all guilty of "locker room talk." In order for a man to respect you, to place you in a category of Unicorn, he has to make an exception to that bias. Let's begin by digging into the root of why so many men will push you aside and leave you confused.

Power Over Women

How Do You Take Away A Woman's Power?
By Making Her Feel Guilty for Having It.

The vast majority of men are in the business of lowering your standards in order to gain power and control over your mind. Chopping a woman down to his size ensures that he will always have a shot at winning you over no matter the situation. Guys with money or good looks can't have a monopoly on the top shelf women. The average man needs to be able to not only get the girl of his dreams but keep her tied to him. This is where the reverse psychology of guilting comes into play. The propaganda of it's totally fine that he's struggling to figure out what he wants in life, that he brings nothing to the table, and that he expects you to hold him down, is framed by "that's what a real woman does because she's not a gold digger." **Men mindfuck women with guilt to create an environment of selflessness.** You're not supposed to be shallow and want good looking guys, you're not supposed to be spoiled and want men that make as much money as you do or more, and you're supposed to put half, if not more, of your own money up during the dating process or you're a ho. "Let me take out my debit card, I don't want him thinking I'm that type of girl..." What, the type with high standards?

If I say something about how a man should always pay on dates, most men will cry, "Fuck that, it's not about the money we spend. It's the effort." Why? Because they don't want women adopting standards that they will have to then adapt to and follow. If I say something about Netflix and Chill being basic, there's the Xbox Live crew there to remind you that there's nothing wrong with a night in, it's the time he's spending that's most important. Finally, if I talk about how men honestly know in a matter of weeks if a girl is worth being official with or not, guys will pop up with, "Not always, some of us need time to blah blah blah." Are your eyes open yet? If not let me spell it out for you. Men use your kindness to get away with murder because they realize society has conditioned women to be selfless to the point of exploitation.

Potential is a smokescreen that men use to hook women. Think about the perfect mixture of male control—first society makes you feel guilty for wanting men to do for you. Second, they promote the idea of being an independent woman as being 50/50 in terms of who pays for dates. This ties equality to romance when romance and courting is one of the few traditions that should remain. Finally, potential comes into play. A man's words, not his actions, are used as bait. He says he's about to do great things, so that means you should give him a chance, go Dutch on dates, and not expect much in terms of a courtship. If you do make demands, it paints you as stuck up and materialistic, not a "good girl" a man marries. I don't care how independent, successful, or sweet a woman is, the moment she bypasses the age-old process of allowing a man to prove his want for her by dating like a gentleman, she will get played or undervalued.

You must reverse this trend by taking self-inventory of how you date and observing if men are depowering you. There are tons of great guys out here who know how to treat a lady, but you will never reach them if you're giving losers all your time. How many months or years have you wasted with a man who you were giving a chance to show you he was more than what he appeared? How did wasting time with "potential" work out? If you're reading this book, you took a loss or are STILL taking an L with your current man. Fuck potential. Fuck guilt. Fuck being self-less! *You will always take that L when you put He before She.* This isn't a man's fault, he's simply trying to upgrade his stable, it's your fault because you're allowing him to upgrade at your expense!

Dig into your thoughts right now. You feel guilty for wanting what you actually want, so you lower your head and tell yourself it's honorable to settle for less. Fuck honor! Who benefits the most from you having low standards? From you being understanding? From you trying to fix a broken man? From your "stand by him," loyalty? In their world, your pussy should not have a class system, it should be given without working for it, just because they deserve it. Your vagina is not a socialist country! **You have the right to have shallow standards because shallow standards are**

the only way you get high-quality men! I don't care how guilty these broke dudes make you feel; you should only be able to be attained by the best of the best!

Picture This: I want you to visualize yourself as an average man competing in today's world for the love of quality women. Let's call you *Paul the Personal Trainer*. You're fit, handsome, but you don't have much clientele aka you're broke. You have enough money to pay your car note, to maintain rent, buy Jordans, and to go out drinking every now and then, but it's a front. You don't have real money to be spending unless it's a necessity. In order for Paul to get the pretty girls before rival men like Doctors or CEO's sweep in, he has to make himself out to be "worth it in the long run." **Broke men do two things exceptionally well: impregnate and sell dreams.** He's telling you that dates should be shared because he knows he can't afford both you and his Xbox games. He's telling you that home cooked meals and watching Hulu is a real date because his disposable income goes to either drinking or smoking. The moment he hears someone attempt to uplift a female with the idea that "Girls need to aim high," he gets upset and reminds women that it's not all about what a man has right now... Why? Because the moment you women actually aim high, he has to step out of his comfort zone and put in real effort.

When you set your bar high, a man like Paul will either show you he actually thinks enough of you to invest the little he has in trying to reach it or go back to the ratchets who are happy with flavored vodka, Netflix, and Dick. Paul usually wins in the end, because even as a broke personal trainer, he's seen as a catch.

Why do women like you or your friends give guys like Paul a chance? Bingo! The big talk of potential mixed with the lack of options, and the guilt of "am I being too picky." A man like Paul won't respect you enough to ever be a stand-up guy. He never had to earn you, so he doesn't value you! Let's go through a few excuses these men will give you for not dating. One of the counter-arguments is "I'm saving my money." Men over 25 and in poverty don't save money, they spend it on dumb shit! Him taking you to dinner isn't denting his imaginary Goldman Sachs account. A good date costs the same as his sneakers, but the difference is those kicks are a must-have, you're just a have. The point is these types of men would rather make excuses than to make plans with you because with enough guilt you feel it's your duty to give broke guys a shot. Regardless of what man is in your ear trying to convince you to sympathize, there must be a moment where you think, *"Wait, is this fool trying to keep my standards low so he can fuck for free with minimal effort and have me assuming that it will lead to a relationship when he's mentally ready?"* You have to wake the fuck up! Most of you protest about racial, financial, and gender inequality, but in your own life, you're allowing yourself to be fucked over by the biggest oppressors in the world—Men that see you as pussy.

Women control the spreading of legs, but men are the gateway to the relationship. In the end, you can't get into a committed relationship unless a man says, "*yes*," and that's what's at the root of this weak basic bitch behavior. Your entire life is built around getting that guy who you like to like you back enough to where he will only want to be with you. There is so much time spent trying to impress these men, but you don't stop to think that it's the man that should be impressing you. **You shouldn't have to work hard to get a commitment, either you are what he finds impressive or you aren't.** However, the lack of confidence in yourself makes you obsess over things you should do to further prove yourselves. You give up control of your pussy, you do him favors, you show him that you're understanding of his lifestyle, you avoid coming off as high maintenance. Women compromise over and over again, all so they can get a man's approval, failing to realize that he has already decided you're nothing special.

Let's look at guys that are financially well off, they too benefit from the Paul's of the world because once one man lowers you, he can come in flash money, trick a little bit, and have you convinced that you're being valued because girls like you aren't used to being spoiled. So many women come bouncing in my inbox about what a guy spent because they are used to men that are broke or cheap. The new guy understands that by doing the materialistic things that others wouldn't, he gets you fast and easy. **He doesn't have to put in energy, just money, and you're open once again off that P-word—Potential.** *"But why did he take me out so many times and waste all that money when it wasn't guaranteed he'd hit?"* Because it ain't tricking if you got it! You can still be just pussy, even if you rack up a $200 dinner bill and get a birthday gift. It's a hustle that men with bread have mastered. You want to be his princess, so you don't vet that man, you soak up the fantasy, roll over, and give him the world in hopes that he will lock you down. In the end, he grows bored and tosses you aside. Leaving you once again to look to Amazon to find a book about how to win a man back after a breakup. That's sad!

No matter if it's a rich man or a poor man, that thirst to be loved blinds you to the obvious red flags and then transforms into paranoia. You're wondering what kind of girl he likes in terms of looks, so you can become that. What kind of girl he likes in terms of personality, so you can adapt those traits. And what kind of girl wows him as oppose to bores him, so you can guarantee that he doesn't fallback anytime soon. Him Him Him! That's where 9 out of 10 of you are fucking up mentally. In the end, you have to be willing to step back, read his actions, ignore the lies coming out of his mouth, and see the obvious: <u>He doesn't want you!</u>

Men Think Differently!

Most men don't want you, they want to fuck you, know the difference. Assuming that generic acts of kindness are a reflection of genuine interest is a rookie mistake. Phone calls and compliments mean nothing. Time and consistency reveal everything. If he's not showing you what you want to see, then he's showing you what you need to see: Your value is limited in his eyes. You don't need to give someone a second chance to show you that you're a second option. Your self-respect needs to weight more than his potential! So many women fall in love with what a man says he will do and ignore what he's doing presently. Potential can't buy you a cup of coffee, and promises are worth even less. Stop making excuses as to why you're being dumb over dick and start filling these holes! He always wants to hang out and doesn't pressure you for sex— You're open. He brought you a gift and men never get you things just because—You're open. He's popular or famous and he's putting his attention on you—You're open. He listened to you vent when he didn't have to—You're open. Once a man gets you open emotionally, you lose all your power. Act like you've had a man give a fuck about you before and stop getting open off the basics!

To listen to you tell it, you don't need a man for anything, guys don't do anything but lie and cum fast, you're a boss bitch, blah blah blah! Then why are these men able to make you act like a typical bitch the moment they take their attention away? Why are you being petty, why are you crying at night, why are you lurking on his social media, why are you constantly reaching out, why are you going over to see him, WHY DO YOU STILL WANT HIM! How can you be so defensive in your attitude, but so defenseless in your actions? I see the cracks in your armor, and so does every man with half a brain. **We don't want women like you, emotional messes that let us get away with everything.** A female's insecurity glows from a mile away and a smart man knows that a male's love is so important to you because your own love isn't good enough. Males don't have mercy, on the weak, they feast, and you're just another meal.

Despite everything I've written, you want to be the exception to the rule, you want to believe so bad that there must be something real inside of him that feels the same way about you that you feel about him. *...hope is a hell of a drug.* Even when you realize these men don't want you, you refuse to cut them off or even let them go without closure. Women pretend they don't care about who likes them but obsess over it in private. He doesn't call you when he says he will, you hate him, you block him, you make a proclamation that you don't need him... then the next day you unblock him because you know damn well you don't want to miss his call. A guy who keeps playing games, putting you second or third, you don't cut him off; his lack of interest does the opposite, and you become driven to get him to like you the same as he did when you first started talking. Some women can't even let a man fallback in peace, you need to send emails, long ass texts, even handwritten letters that tell the story from your side. Did Adele's ex pick up that phone in "Hello"? No. Will your little friend read any of that crybaby bullshit you're sending him—Fuck No. He'll scan it over, and either stay out of your life or see it as an opening to come back and finish milking your lovesick ass. You don't want closure; you want him to want you back because your ego can't take a man showing you that you're nothing special.

Spartan The Fuck Up!

One day you'll meet a man that will thank the universe that the men before him made the mistake of letting you go. The problem is, you want that man to come right now. You assume you're mentally ready, you swear that you know what you want, but the reality is that you have been in such a rush to get to the finish line of love that you missed the lessons that could have saved you time and energy. Everyone picks wrong before they pick right, it's in those missteps that we gain the wisdom that will lead to better results. When you ignore the lessons and rush into relationship after relationship because you hate the feeling of being alone, you will find yourself repeating the same mistakes with the same type of men. It's your own impatience, fear, and inability to see the bigger picture that will keep you locked in a hell of your own making. No matter how much better than the average woman you believe you are, you will be humbled by a man who comes in, mind fucks you, and shows you that you aren't as ahead of the curve as your ego gassed you to believe. It's happened to everyone from JLo to Oprah, they chose wrong early, so they could smarten up and choose right later in life. I know that you have to hold on to this idea that you're the exception to the rule, the girl who will hit a home run her first time at bat. A few of you truly will be the exception, but for the vast majority of you will be baptized by the fire of getting played. Most of the men you meet will be nothing more than a LESSON.

The right man will sweep you off your feet and make you believe that he's the opposite of what I write about. I get it all the time, *"GL, I met a guy and he's so different, he challenges me, we click spiritually... blah blah fucking blah."* And my advice is to slow down, and take it step by step to be sure. But no one takes advice when things are going good. Being a Spartan doesn't mean you won't make an occasional mistake. The point isn't to not get burnt, the point is to learn and adapt <u>after</u> you get burnt. Most women ask, *"why did this happen"* or *"how can I get it back to where it was."* Dating is rarely about fixing him or fixing what he said was your problem so you two can restart. It's about discovering your strengths and weaknesses so that you evolve, not hang on to that man, go back to him, be on and off, or replace him with someone with the same qualities.

Time is only your enemy when you refuse to learn the lessons that will prevent you from wasting even more time. Stop being so dramatic every time something doesn't work out and recognize that the universe is clearing the way for something better! You don't get everything you want, but once you end up with what you always needed, you will realize that past want was fool's gold. Let go of this want to make a man love you, take you back, or see you as a Unicorn. Embrace the journey that will lead to the one you were always meant for, that kindred spirit who will never ask you to change, surrender, or dumb down your True self.

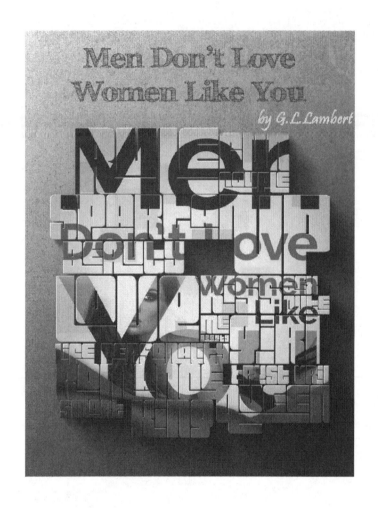

MDLWLY
Bonus Chapter:

Stuck! How to Spartan Up in 3 Days

"We are on a journey of becoming that which we already are.
That is the impossible paradox of our lives."
–Leonard Jacobson

ou were doing great, and then you got stuck. You met a man, went through a life crisis, or maybe you just sank into old thoughts and lost your Spartan mindset. This chapter is a **3 Day Crash Course** that will get you back to the center of your power and keep you there. There is a woman who I will call Monica, that read Chapter 5 of this book and briefly awoke from her dream. She finally felt as if everything made sense. Her so-called bad luck, her defensive attitude, the depression she had struggled with since college, even her on again off again boyfriend of the past three years, she conquered them. By understanding herself through the words on those pages, she was able to step back from her old worldview, cast off her fragile ego, and admit that it was all her creation. She wrote me a lengthy email filled with excitement about her progress. Almost a month later Monica returned to me, having retreated into the shell of her former self the moment her ex-boyfriend started calling again, asking for another chance. All her old anxieties came roaring back and the success she had those first weeks were soon forgotten because she allowed her old way of thinking to trip up her new way of living. Monica crashed back down into typical behavior. She was quick to blame the man for taking her off her square, for putting stress back in her life, and that next email was all about—him him him.

When I reminded Monica about the lessons of the book and her own admission that a man can't force himself into a woman's life, he has to be let in, she replied, "It's easier said than done." Like Monica, most of you may be tested, and you may relapse back into the life of a typical that places blame on others as if they are the center of your universe. He did this to you, she said this about you, nothing is working out because the world is against you. To have read *Men Don't Love Women Like You*, in its entirety and still place blame on external forces, means that you didn't understand it at all. This chapter is for all of the Monica's out there, a kick in the ass reminder that if you want consistent results, you have to not only think, but live like a Spartan consistently, or you will always revert back to your old Placeholder life.

Everything is easier said than done when you don't have mental discipline. When an undisciplined person takes their perfectly formed intentions and positive thoughts and goes out into the world to exercise their will, something happens to sabotage all of the work they have done— they second guess themselves. *Spartan Up, be confident, go conquer!* You can reply with an enthusiastic "Yes, sir" but as soon as you put this book down and my words no longer fill your head, you stumble. A moment ago, you had the courage to eye fuck a stranger, to walk up and introduce yourself in a crowded room, or to tell someone you have been crushing on that you're interested. Now, your confidence buckles as you imagine negative outcomes. The keyword being, "imagine."

When you embraced Spartanhood, you saw how silly fear is and how the concept of rejection makes people timid, in effect limiting their success in all walks of life. The truth of your power over your reality has been made crystal clear in the previous chapters, but now that it's time to put those things into action, you flinch. "What if" once again returns and instead of moving with conviction and confidence, you turtle into a shell waiting for a "sign" that you should go forward with all this Spartan stuff. What if that stranger thinks your eye fuck is stupid. What if you walk up to a guy and he laughs in your face? What if you tell your friend you're trying to be more than just friends and he awkwardly replies that he doesn't see you that way. That would crush you. How could you look yourself in the mirror the next day knowing that you failed again after all that talk about how you were a warrior queen? So here you are again, back to a normal fear-based human. Just another person that lets their thoughts control them and lead them into the perpetual state of "I don't know what to do." The irony is that you now know what to do and how to do it! Push the fear of failure from your mind and embrace confidence as if you can't lose, and you won't lose. Get over the past in the ways listed earlier and start anew without pointing to some old insecurity as a reason for an imagined future failure. You know what it takes to move to the next level, but you doubt yourself and skip the process. You love all this Spartan stuff in theory, but you're far too afraid to actually do it because of those "What if" fears that crowd your mind and cripple your actions the moment you try to do these things as opposed to just read about them. You aren't stuck, you're holding back.

This book is not for readers, it's for practitioners. Life is made up of two types of people, cowards that sit on the sideline, sporadically taking safe chances and winners that stand on the front lines and understand that even when things don't go according to plan, it's still going according to a higher plan. This chapter is meant to stamp out the last bit of weak bitch that resides in you. That soft, counter-thought having, non-believing, excuse making, negative part of you has to go for your life to change. You've come this far don't you want the results? You've spent hours reading and internalizing, are you really going to let nerves nullify that? I don't want you to read this book and say, "that was good advice it made me feel better," I want you to do better! This is it, your last chance to get this right now as opposed to later. I do not care if you enjoy this book as a work of entertainment, I am only concerned with you using this book as a tool to conquer your fears, upgrade your thinking, and visibly change your life instantly! If you have hit a wall where you feel stuck, confused, or are having a crisis of faith because being a Spartan is overwhelming and running contrary to your old weak programming, then pause your mission right here and take this crash course in destroying that negativity. No matter if this is your first time reading this or your 22nd time reading it, come here when you feel lost, and the path will be relit.

Think of this as dipping your toe in the water of enlightenment. I don't want you to drown in all the ideas and revelations of this book, so let's take this day by day— literally. If you've gotten lost or just need a refresher, then hit reset by going through this process for 3 DAYS. Be patient and don't rush. If you feel as if you didn't do Day 1 right, go back and do it again. If you need more time before going on to Day 2, take it. It's better to do these things the right way than to just skim through as if you're studying for a test like, "yeah, I got it," only to race off and stumble again. Actually get it by spending an entire day focused on one step and one step only.

Day 1 – Stay Out of Your Old Head

Spartan you, your current state of mind, is not chained to the past actions of your former self. The mistakes of the past, the shame of the past, and the outcomes of past situations that formed this mental image of your character have to be looked back on like infancy, with detachment. You can look at baby pictures and call it "me," but mentally the lights were off, it was you in a sense, but that wasn't your True Self. The same way a person looking at their baby pictures can't relate to how it felt, a Spartan looking back at a previous life has to become just as removed. We don't carry the guilt of throwing toys or food at our parents during a hissy fit as a two-year-old. Even when we're old enough to know right from wrong, we don't carry the guilt of breaking the house rules as a 7-year-old because we are given the excuse of "they are just growing up and acting out," and forgiven fairly quickly. As a teenager, you continued to make mistakes that you learned from, but the guilt started to stick under the shame of "I should have known better." The guilt of not living up to your parent's expectations, not following a rule, or choosing a path that ended in you making a mistake, builds to a boil like a tea kettle. No one tells you to forgive yourself nor do they explain that even the wrong moves are the right moves in retrospect.

You live with this overwhelming feeling that you can't mess up again, that your future is at stake, that you have to follow certain rules, or you will fail. By carrying that fear of ruining your life or letting someone down, you apply unfair pressure that keeps that tea kettle at a boil. Teenage you, young adult you, even fully adult you, was just as ignorant as the infant version of you. It's only through becoming smarter and ascending mentally do you realize all of that shit that you saw as negative was simply the process of you learning to walk. How can you judge yourself when you were so misinformed about life? This isn't about the lack of responsibility for your past, it's about reframing the past as a roadmap that always leads you to the same point in life—the awakening.

"I wish I would have told that person I liked them... I wished I would have picked a different school... I wish I could go back and do over everything that didn't work out as expected..." You make-believe that you had options, but the truth is there was only ONE PATH, the one you took that led you right here. Going off into this fantasy of what could have been creates this imagined life that's better than the one you are living today. **You could be filthy rich right now if you did this, you could be happily married right now if you did that... it's all pretend**. The result of looking down on yourself based on a perceived wrong move or a series of mistakes is depression. Instead of focusing on your actual life, you're escaping into the fantasy of, "I messed everything up back in the day, now it's all ruined, what's the point..." Shame, guilt, and pity all based on some bullshit turning point where your life went astray from some destined path. I repeat, there was only one path to take, and you took it. You were sleepwalking through a story; you can't judge new you for the actions of ignorant old you. The mental image of who you think you are, the one who made bad choices, who acted petty, who fell into a category of being just as typical as the next person, how much of that was the True Self and how much of it was you being on autopilot?

****

Let's go back to why you can't get over the hump even when confronted with the truth. The mind has a nasty habit of reminiscing on the bad things that have happened, the missed opportunities, or the mistakes you've made and it projects that not as a prolog, but as a cycle that you're stuck in. For instance, if you were cheated on as a teenager, the fear that it's going to happen again is always there. No matter what circumstantial excuse you made in order to push it to the back of your mind or how many times you claim to be over it, your personality has been traumatized to the point where the idea of being cheated on is part of your DNA. The reality that you created is one where a man cheated on you because you lacked something, which means there is still something about you that would make a man cheat again. All of the fragile affirmations about what happened not being about you work fine when you're alone, but they don't hold up when you are actually in a relationship. Those "he's going to get bored... I'm just not good enough..." thoughts rush back, and you are once again nervous and afraid that this new man, who is showing nothing but positive signs, will hurt you. A girl once told me, "I don't know why I keep dwelling on him possibly cheating on me, I know it's all in my head." The reason that phobia never dies out is because you don't see a separation in character from who you once were and who you now are after understanding the truth of this game you call life. You can literally change the direction of where your life has been heading by reframing and rewriting, but how can you do any of those things if you're stuck in the negative head space of your past life?

Day 1 is all about focusing on the difference between past and present. It's extremely important to create a breaking point as opposed to a split personality. You can't be half Spartan and half Basica and expect to get consistent results. **Confidence built on a false foundation isn't actually confidence, it's delusion**. Try to Spartan up while skipping the part where you reframe and build true self-esteem, and you will revert to the old you the moment the pressure of a conversation or a situation you didn't plan for emerges. Evolving isn't about forgetting or about lying to yourself. It's about understanding and forgiving the mistakes of the past because you weren't operating at 100%. Why would a man not want you as a girlfriend, another female not want you as a friend, or a boss not want to promote you? There was something you were lacking! A man who rejected you last year was rejecting a weak, watered-down version of who you truly are. A best friend who started distancing herself from you was rejecting a flawed version of who you truly are. At work, that wasn't Spartan you, that was Slave you, that's why you weren't respected. Drill the difference between last year's you and this moment's you into your psyche!

Look back on how you used to act at every step in your life, and it will point to instances where you think nostalgically, "Wow, I can't believe I used to be that way." The moment you open your eyes to your own ignorant or misinformed ways, you automatically morph into a new person who would never act in that way again. You can't go back and redo life, you can't live with regret over choices already made, but you can recognize that life starts anew the moment you separate autopilot mode from this manual mode. Today you begin your mission by creating a unified you, a Spartan mind void of the past baggage which keeps you overthinking your moves and repeating the same old mistakes. *Old you would do this, Spartan you would do that, but what is the right way?* That battle has to end, there is only one way of thinking—the Spartan Way.

Step 1 – Old Vs. New: From the time you wake up I want you to have dual thoughts. The first thought is your Basica mind, indecisive, pessimistic, worried, and living in a world where everything is chaos and out of your control. The second thought is your Spartan mind, strong, determined, positive, in on the secret that this is your world. When you wake up, take a moment to reflect on this new day from both sides. The Basica version of you would think what? She would worry about being late for school or work, maybe get annoyed that she has to get up while still being sleepy or become overwhelmed by the stress of the day that's not even started. Basic minds are always pointed towards the negative aspects of everyday life. Think about that person who made you mad the day before who you may have to see or talk to today. Think about the clothes you either picked out last night or are about to pick out, and how they aren't good enough. Think about any and every source of frustration or annoyance that a normal person would think about right after hitting their alarm clock. Got it? Now revert to your Spartan Mind.

Laugh it off. It's all one big joke. This is a world that you created, where you are living out this story as the only aware character who knows it's all just a soap opera. Think about how stupid that stress of the Basic mind now seems. Why would you wake up thinking about another person? They're the supporting character, you're the main character. Fuck them. The more you feed into the worry of seeing a person you have a problem with or getting a text from someone that's making you mad, the larger the part you will give them in your day. Why didn't such and such text you back, why did such and such get smart with you yesterday, all these dumb ass why's no longer matter. You must crush the idea that someone else can affect your mood, or they will continue to influence your world. Why would you stress about something as stupid as what to wear? Because you're worried about how everyone will judge you if you don't look your best. Fuck their opinions, again you're falling into the trap of outside opinion, and that will relapse you. Do you look good? Did you actually follow one of the first rules of Spartanhood and fall in love with that mirror or did you brush that off like a weak, undisciplined phony? If you love that person in the mirror, then you can wear a potato sack and still feel attractive. The clothes don't make the woman; the woman makes the clothes.

A Spartan's mind in the morning is one of excitement. You literally just woke up in a fucking video game designed for your ascension! Why would you worry about being late or running into someone you don't want to see when every choice you will make from now on is going to be a positive one? If life is leading you to be late, fuck it, be late! This may be the day where those extra five minutes leads to you running into someone or something that may change your story for the better. Everyone has those moments where they say, "If I would have taken my normal route, I would have missed out on..." or "If I would have done things as planned I would have ended up in the same bad situation as..." Instead of allowing the pressure of your day to force you to react like a chicken with its head cut off, calm down. If you feel as if everything you're doing is going wrong, then stop fighting against the tide and live in the moment. Instead of rushing, relax. Instead of letting external frustration shift your mood, slow your breathing, remember who you are, and neutralize the negativity. No matter what event is happening at the start of your day put it in perspective. There are no such things as bad days, just bad thoughts! There are scenarios where you can't physically change what's going on, but you can mentally change them by shifting your view from negative to positive, from hopeless to hopeful, and from fear to confidence!

Carry this morning process over as you leave the house and deal with others. Remember, that until you can actually face the outside world with the same knowledge and confidence in which you face the internal world, it's all theory. Walking outside is your first real test. You don't need to visualize a perfect day or say, "Lord, let everything go right." That's the mind of a fearful person who feels their game of life is out of their control and being guided by some other force. You are the force. So long as your Spartan Mind is soaked in positivity, everything will fall into place without wishing or praying. The Basica Mind would go out in public and become quickly annoyed because as the old cliché goes "she got up on the wrong side of the bed." Bad traffic, people who didn't shower, someone stepping on your shoes, a news story about some kind of injustice... all of these things put weak minded people in foul moods that they carry around with them all day. Face screwed up because you're annoyed, voice aggressive because you're frustrated, conversation negative because all you want to talk about is how someone or something upset you that morning. That's how Basica always thinks, she is reactionary and a slave to her environment, not a creator. Switch to your Spartan Mind and stop looking at other people as obstacles or annoyances, and to see them for what they truly are—you.

Step 2 – Understanding Projections: *Thoughts create reality* is the hardest thing to understand, and I don't expect you to comprehend it until you actually go out and see it for yourself. During your day, pay attention to your thoughts then pay attention to your environment so you can directly see your thoughts in action. Other people will either uplift you or annoy you. It's your choice in terms of what you let in and what you discard as noise. Your mind is a factory of negative and positive thoughts. At this stage you aren't having strictly positive thoughts. Therefore, you won't have strictly positive projections. To overcome your own counterproductive thoughts turned real-life manifestations, you have to learn to let go of people and things that are trying to push your buttons. Someone says something to annoy you about your looks or about your behavior, let it go, don't feed it. Something happens such as bad news or a random accident, don't stew in that place of negativity, take it in, dissect the events, but let go of the negativity that would normally create pity or anger.

A Spartan doesn't allow the buzzing about of flies affect her mood. This doesn't mean stay neutral and numb like an emotionless robot, it means step back and look at those things you see as conflict or stress, as part of a current story based on your recent mood. Not your current mood, your recent mood, understand the difference. Let's say that you're already in a counter state of mind from the day before or even the week before, you're okay on the surface, but you are still thinking about those past annoyances. You can't start thinking positively or highly at 8am and have it translate by noon. Like a bank transfer, it often takes time to process before it shows up.

Your day is already being determined by your habitual thoughts of negativity and stress. Therefore, during this first day, take back your power by not feeding into the current projections of negativity. You don't need to confront gossip. You don't need to have the last word in an argument. You don't need to prove yourself to anyone today. Let's be honest, the power placed in the hands of other people is enormous. You say things like, "I hope they don't make me mad... I hope they're in a good mood... I hope such and such doesn't get on my nerves..." before a situation happens you're already projecting this idea that someone is going to act in a negative way that will, in turn, make you feel negative. To go on lunch and text people about what someone is doing to you or to go home that night and retell a story about who pissed you off, what does that show? It shows that you were affected, that it still is bothering you, and it ensures that the next day will be more of the same because your mind is already projecting tomorrow's frustration, today!

In addition to people in the flesh, those on the internet, be it social media chatter or news stories, can also project things that will place you in a negative space. Don't allow electronics to distract or shift your mood. You could be happy and keep seeing funny memes. You could be lonely and keep seeing relationship quotes. You could be angry and keep seeing crime stories. There will also be patterns of things that constantly pop up based on not only your current attitude but your constant attitude and views. Don't let it lead you one way or another mentally. No matter if it's a story about what a politician said, some murder committed, or celebrity gossip, look beyond the normal vantage point of a sleepwalker. Not for some hidden sign that relates to your current life story, but in a way where you understand that it's all just a show meant to get you to react. **Synchronicity between you and your world is always in effect**. If you're in a bad mood, you're popping bad things into your world in the form of people, news, or various other media. If you're obsessing over a person or thing, you're popping them or things that remind you of them into your world. Again, your mind is a schism of dark and light throughout the day, but ask yourself what part has the most control?

One minute it's "believe, and you can achieve" the next it's "People are holding me back!" Which is it? That's determined by what you truly feel. This world isn't a chaotic mess unless you want to believe that it's a chaotic mess. You invent the positive as well as the negative. Choose to see life as your diverse playground as opposed to a scary prison and watch how the universe begins to morph. Everything is dependent on your outlook! Crybaby or conquer, that's up to you.

Some believe that the solution to feeling better about life is external, not internal. They look to people and images as mood motivators, but ask yourself what does that actually solve? Anyone can look at a happy image or get a compliment and feel good for a moment. If your entire day is built around things changing your mood both good and bad, who is really in control of your life? Your internal is determining your external. One feeds the other in an infinite cycle. That doesn't mean that a positive life only showcases positive images, variety is necessary, but you will be amazed by the things that you no longer see or hear about the more you focus less on the bad and more on the great. By the end of this day, you will start feeling lighter because you're unbothered, not fake unbothered where you just suppress your feelings and pretend as if you're good but truly unaffected by outside forces. Stay in your Spartan Mindset for the rest of the day and come tomorrow you may not see 100% positive new projections, but you will see a huge change from the day before. The key is to maintain this way of thinking day after day no matter what pops up that threatens to relapse you. I promise that if you stay the course, the daily routine of last Friday compared to this Friday will seem like you hit the lottery. Trust in the process. The more your mind is free of tension and worry the less and less you will have people popping into your story with unhealthy drama.

Step 3 – The First Chapter Test: At the end of Day 1, I want you to write something down. It can be on paper or in your phone's notes, doesn't matter so long as you can go back to it for reference. You just went through a day as Spartan (*insert your Spartan name here*) that was your character and today was chapter one of her story. I want you to write out what this Spartan did today as if you were writing a Children's Book, meaning make it simple and easy to follow. Doesn't have to be a fancy novel, doesn't need proper grammar and spelling, this is for your eyes only so you can reflect. Begin with: *Today Spartan _____ woke up and...* Lay out your activities no matter how boring or routine. The purpose of this final exercise is to force you to look back while in the now of your True Self and see that this day and every day before it isn't this scary, frustrating chaos, it's merely a story you're projecting dependent on thought. Detach yourself when you write, don't use the word "I" use your Spartan name as if you're simply the narrator writing down her tale.

When you finish writing her story, ask yourself what you could do to make her story more interesting. Maybe tomorrow you want her to try someplace different for lunch. Maybe tomorrow you want her to skip school or work and go to the zoo. It doesn't matter what it is, think about the story you just wrote and ask yourself how can you make her life more fulfilling or entertaining. This is who you are, the master of this universe that chooses, not reacts. You're not the character that woke up this morning and ran around, you're the one deciding that character's path with the insight that it's your amusement park.

Do you understand what your Spartan Thoughts were now? They were your out of body reflections that can overpower your Basica Mind. You are operating the body of a Warrior Queen by using Goddess Consciousness. There is nothing to fear, no one that can hold you back or break you, and no more mistakes to be made once you are firmly operating at this higher level! Look at the story you just wrote, that's her life that you are making her live. The world she's operating in isn't under the control of some outside force. Yes, it has rules like any game in terms of the physics and science of how things operate and move, but it is your playground to explore. The Universe you've created will never be vanilla. You cannot truly experience the game of life if there were world peace, everyone had the same amount of money, bigotry didn't exist, and people weren't messy or conniving. Imagine watching *The Walking Dead*, and everyone got along, sitting through *Empire* with no backstabbing, or playing *Mario Kart* where everyone neatly raced around the track. That shit would be boring! The world you exist in is rich in experiences that push you to develop new skills that ultimately lead you to new opportunities that promote mental growth and will lead to a higher evolution.

All of this bullshit about what guy likes you, what girl doesn't like you, not having enough money, it all becomes laughable once you truly grasp who you are. The seemingly chaotic backdrop and interpersonal tensions are what makes all of this fun. The problem with the Basica Mind is that it is always in a state of worry that things won't work out in the end. This feeling that everything is bad, people are out to get you, or you can die any moment, keep weak minds depressed and miserable. They aren't playing the game, they are a victim of the game, that is why they will always struggle. Look once again at the story you just wrote, if you aren't happy with that day to day, then you can change it tomorrow in any way you want. You spent years growing, learning, being pulled into all kinds of directions, being told what to think about everything, and now with a clear mind of a Spartan, you must become self-aware that you are the Universe. Once you control your thoughts, you will then be able to control your reactions, and because you understand the randomness of the world is a mirage, you can appreciate the game for what it is...

STOP! Continue to Day 2 tomorrow

The Unicorn Delusion:

Day 2 – Observe & Engage with Others

Yesterday was about understanding your thoughts, today is about exercising your will. Thinking that this is your world and knowing it isn't the same concept and won't net real results. I am not asking you to take anything written in this book on faith alone. Everything must be done. By doing you prove. By proving, you erase all doubts. Knowing this works 100% and consistently will give you the confidence to take bigger and bigger steps until you have literally mastered your universe. There are so many voices pushing you to simply believe, fuck that! I want you to know through proof of your own actions so no internal or external force can ever cast doubt. Before we get into today's steps, you need to confront two emotions: Insecurity & Jealousy. Before you suck your teeth and proclaim that you're neither of these things, let's go past the words and truly define what they mean beyond your personal semantics.

I talk a lot about flirting, going for the person you want via seduction, and using conversation to break down a person's agenda. That sounds good in theory, right? Yet most women freeze up in practice. A stumbling block that's been brought to my attention is the fear of other people. You may be naturally shy, or you may only become shy when around other people who you feel are intimidating. Today's exercise is meant to destroy that fear for good. Let's focus on insecurity first. On the surface you may feel secure, but how do know if that's true internally? If things are going great during your Spartan journey until you have to interact with other people, then you still have insecurity buried inside. Why should you fear another person when they are nothing more than a projection? **Because you don't believe that they are a projection**. You are so locked into the idea that you are merely a player in the game that you remain at the mercy of background characters.

You see a rich man as better than you because of his money. You see a smart man as better than you because of his intelligence. You see a handsome man as better than you because you imagine he could get a woman that looks prettier than you. How can you interact with someone on an even level, let alone a higher level, if you're assuming that you aren't up to their standards? It's impossible. Stuttering, not being able to get the right words out, saying something redundant or corny, awkwardly making eye contact only to look away... You have no problem talking to friends and zero anxiety when intermingling with people you see as normal. However, when interacting with those you felt were superior or strangers who you feared were going to judge, the old way of thinking caused you to lock up. You didn't want to say anything dumb or lacking in wit and be laughed at. You didn't want to show a lack of class and refinement and seem like a peasant pretending to be fancy. You definitely didn't want to show interest in an attractive man only to be rejected because you weren't his type. Fear won out and shrunk your confidence. You shot yourself in the foot, punked out, and filtered your personality based on your own insecurity. The more insecure you felt, the more negative your projections were. Of course you blew it, of course they weren't interested, you already determined that by opening your mouth with fear as opposed to confidence! That circle of negative attraction based on your own internal feelings of insecurity played out day after day. Not anymore. Yesterday was all about dealing with those old thoughts, today is about confronting them directly.

How can the sun be inferior to the planets in the solar system?

Let's take a hard look at jealousy. Much like insecurity, people claim they are above this emotion with defensive cries of, "What do I have to be jealous of?" There are levels to jealousy, not just the token examples of envy. In your old life, there were people who had more than you in one area or another. You can't lie to yourself and say that you never wished for something based off seeing someone else with it. Those feelings didn't die; they were buried and, in most cases, only came out when confronted with someone who had what you wanted. Prefacing things with, "I'm not hating but," or coming up with a special treatment excuse for why someone is in a position or has something are all products of your internal frustrations. Regardless if you say them, think them, or simply laugh along and co-sign when someone else chimes in with shade, it reflects back to you. Let's sidestep those angry emotions and take a look at the other side of jealousy that no one talks about, the kind that leads to inferiority.

The inferiority that you feel being around other people that are more interesting, more popular or those who command more attention is a product of repressed envy. A woman once told me that she passed the Bar exam, posted about it on Facebook, only to see the girl she grew up with post about a job as a Stewardess get triple the likes. She asked me, "does it make me a bad person that I let her likes bother me?" Jealousy is an imagined feeling that other people are luckier, more blessed, more special, or generally more successful than you in areas where you feel you are lacking. One of the conditioned human lies is telling yourself that you're humble while secretly wishing for attention. You graduated but didn't get as many congratulations as you expected. You had a birthday but didn't get as many gifts as you assumed you would. You achieved something great, but the recognition someone else got for something not nearly as important was far greater than yours. You are that girl with the Facebook post, feeling less important. In reality, you must become the sun, no fucks given about the planets, because in the end, they all revolve around you!

You can't participate in Day 2 if your main thoughts are, "I want what they have...why not me." I am going to send you out into your world to imprint your will, but how can you Spartan up if you're afraid of other people or using the crutch of social anxiety? Stop limiting yourself! If you give into social anxiety, then you're admitting to yourself that this isn't your world and handing over your power to your environment. The more you feel you lack, the more you will lack. The more you hate on others, the more you hate yourself. You don't have to be jealous of anyone, make excuses as to why someone has something you don't, or use the illogical excuse that, "If I were the master of this universe I'd have everything in the world at the snap of a finger." This is your ascension story, not some childhood fantasy where you start off with all the toys and attention. Everything in your life is there for a reason, you put it there. Stop giving into petty feelings of desire, materialistic cravings, and any other ego fueled feelings because you are about to see how easy it is to live a life where you will never want for anything ever again.

Now that your mind is clear from the contradiction of insecurity and the internal whispers of jealousy, I want you to hit pause on the game and observe it through the eyes of the Goddess you are. Watch, Listen and Interact with your subjects. Today you conquer the fear of being shy and dismiss the paranoia that comes with the possibility of rejection. The observing portion can be done outside, or you can observe people online or on TV. However, the interacting can only be done outside. Yes, you have to go outside and interact with people. I repeat, this book is for you to put into practice, not sit on your ass and talk about, "It sounds good, I get it." Practical application is a must! Last night you wrote the story of "her" down. Today you are actively in control of the story and where you take it. Let's begin.

Step 1 – The Watcher: From the time you wake up, watch people from the perspective of the person with the joystick, not the character playing the game. Look at how people walk, the way they make eye contact, the little nervous ticks they do, from stroking their hair to tapping their fingers. Notice how people vary in their own confidence. Take note of how they awkwardly or over-confidently play their parts. From the mailman to the gardener, all the way to your co-worker or best friend. Observe them silently and think one thing, "they're extras in my movie…" Don't focus on the things they say right now, just look through them and see them the same way you see an actor playing a waiter in a Jennifer Lopez movie. These people, be they online or in your personal space, aren't better than you, smarter than you, or more attractive than you. They are you. Pieces of you playing a role to make your life an experience. Stay in this mindset for the rest of the day.

Step 2 – The Listener: How can you flirt, banter, debate, or even seduce if you are second guessing every word that comes out of your mouth for fear of sounding dumb or uninteresting? You can't! I want you to listen to people and how they talk. The words they stumble on when excited, the flow of their sentences, their bad grammar, even their misuse of words or phrases. Humanize people by realizing that everyone who is talking, even when confident, isn't perfect. The guy at work who you have a crush on, you may see him as cool and collected, but listen with your ears, not the bias of your eyes, and you will hear the cracks in his voice, the rushed thoughts, and the hesitations before opening his mouth. The athlete or celebrity on TV doing an interview, even if it's been edited together you can see them fumbling for the right words, overthinking too much, the nerves rolling off their tongue. Everyone in your world can be stripped away of their perfection the moment you look deeper into their actions as opposed to over-analyzing your own flaws. Listen to them instead of listening to your own internal thoughts about them judging you or being superior, and you will see through their act the same way a great actor can see through an amateur's performance.

Step 3 – The Talker: If you watch people long enough in public you notice a pattern. Did you see it today? If not take another day to do the first part of this exercise over. This has to be experienced not read about. If you listen to people talk directly to you with a clear mind, you can get a feel for their mood, be it nervous, excited, inquisitive, doesn't matter. Everyone can be broken down. You have family members whose habits you know by heart, correct? You can tell when someone is going to ask for a favor by how they breathe and start a sentence. You can tell when someone has bad news by how they struggle to spit it out or try to preface it with nonsense chit-chat. You can tell when a close friend is nervous or upset without them even saying a word. The same is true of strangers if you develop this gift. The ability to predict people is a huge "ah-ha" moment. When you are placed in situations that aren't foreign in terms of conversation with a person you aren't intimidated by, it leads to you feeling comfortable enough to speak up, joke, be witty, or converse in any manner you want. Having confidence in your conversation is something the vast majority of women lack when talking to new men. Reading men is the key to seeing them as human, harmless, and extremely malleable.

Let's say you're talking to a male, doesn't matter if you are attracted to him or not, you would most likely talk to him differently from how you would talk to a woman because you feel as if you have to project a certain image for his approval. Women have been led to feel as if a man's attention is golden, and that has obviously lead to this nervous feeling of doubt: *Am I pretty enough for him... Smart enough for him... funny enough for him...* Females objectify themselves based on how men will objectify them. How you come off is more about a man's expectations than your actual personality. In reality, you aren't afraid to be goofy, eat like a pig, and make inappropriate jokes. Your friends get to see that side. However, around men an act is put on. Never again. A Spartan does not perform for male approval; she makes him perform for her approval by using the tools we developed today. You watched how people act, you listened to how they talk, you understand that there is nothing "scary" about people, especially men. Using this knowledge, you can shake off this idea of being shy and redefine how he sees you by using your words to lead his mind.

What does a man think when he's in front of you? If he's sexually or romantically interested he thinks one thing, "**I have to get her to like me**." That's it. While Basicas are sweating bullets trying to gain acceptance they fail to realize that men are even more pressured to perform because they want to see you naked! That means as a woman, you have power over any man that is attracted to you. To ask him a question that isn't easy to answer will make that man nervous, he will rush for an answer, maybe dart his eyes around if you're making strong eye contact because he can't think under that pressure. To give him a compliment on his clothes or appearance will disarm him because he now feels you like him back. Try it out, give a man a compliment on his eye color or smile. He will rush to shoot you a thank you, look for something smooth, witty, or funny to say in response, or he may be taken off guard and fidget for a response. The point is, that when you slow down human interaction and make conversations less scary, you can see a man's mind working. The more you talk to people, the more transparent they become. It's only when you make a man bigger than human that you become the one rushing your words, struggling for a topic, and being led by their charm. The task at hand is simple: Lead a conversation with confidence. The biggest trip up is usually, "what do I say to him," when you see a guy in public or when you are on your first date. I can sit and tell you to feel powerful, but if your mind says, "I get it, just tell me what I have to say, because I don't know what words to use," then you haven't been paying attention. There is no script to follow because you're writing it as you go by watching, listening, and deciding the right way to go in at him. Let me show you how this works.

Pick someone of the opposite sex to start a conversation with today. They don't have to be a stranger, but they have to be someone who isn't a close friend who you feel totally comfortable around. Look at a man's eyes when he speaks to you, don't shy away like some little girl. Are his eyes locked on yours? Do they shy away from yours? Then you have him open. Does his voice have an inflection of excitement? Are his words jumbling together in a rush? Then you have him open. His cheeks puffing up to hide his grin, a smile that won't leave, body language leaning into you, or the touching of your hand or shoulder, they all tell you that you have him on the hook. Today is all about getting a man on the hook. This doesn't mean you have to give him your number or take his number or even say anything romantic. The goal is to start a conversation randomly and push it in a direction where you want. I don't care if you walk up to a maintenance worker and get him talking about a TV show or if you walk up to a guy sitting at a bar and get him talking about his favorite color. I want you to prove to yourself that it's easy to talk to any man about anything and that this fear of rejection is much ado about nothing.

Of course, there will be fish you have to through back, men who don't make eye contact and seem distracted. A man whose voice is monotone without much engagement. Fidgeting body language that comes across as distancing, will not be hard to see after you do these steps. To talk to a man that isn't responsive doesn't mean you aren't doing it right, the mission is about you feeling comfortable not him being interested. Again, if he's boring or dry, end the conversation and try with someone else until you find a man you can get on the hook. Once you have a man on the hook, gut him with your words. No longer should you be afraid to joke, to laugh, to poke fun at him, or to use sexual innuendo to flirt. He's already showing you that he's more nervous than you are. Go for broke. I repeat, don't go out looking to get a number, just talk to a grown man and hold a conversation. This can be five minutes or forty minutes, but it must be done in person. No texting or Video chats, I want you to face your fear of locking eyes and having to go back and forth with a dialogue.

Again, if he's unresponsive, then it's a good reason, not proof that you're not pretty enough to talk to or interesting enough to converse with. Don't backtrack into your old thoughts. Someone doesn't talk back, so what, on to the next. There can be no more of this defeatist attitude or fear that you can't do it; if you believe you can you will! I don't want to hear the excuse that there were no men to talk to when the mission wasn't "find a cute man" it was to find any man. Get this done, don't punk out! By the end of the day, you will see through the mask of people and understand just how easy it is to use your words to dissect them even further.

STOP! Continue to Day 3 tomorrow

Day 3 – Embrace The Truth Through Meditation

Day 1 you were forced to analyze your thoughts and live in the moment instead of being on autopilot. Day 2 you were forced to pay attention to other people, to defang them, and finally face your fears by starting and holding a conversation with someone you didn't really know. By the third day, I don't expect you to be a master your thoughts and actions, but I do expect you to be back on track. It only took 48 hours to see how fear and ignorance had you operating at 50% of your potential and limiting the experiences you could be having. It's so easy to forget everything you learn when you step back into your day to day life. This way of thinking, supremely and confidently, is new to you, hence, there will be times when you doubt your power. Other times you may hypnotize yourself; become so caught up in the game that you forget that it's a game. Right now, you're snapped out of the trance, you have seen through the veil and you're secure in your truth, but that confidence will fade the longer you go without revisiting the truth of self.

This is why meditation is the most important of all of these steps. No matter how busy your life becomes, meditation remains the most convenient tool there is to anchor you. There will be times when you take a week off from living in the now, get caught up in the drama at work, have finals at school, or experience tragedy in your life that makes you question everything. During these events you won't be thinking about this being your universe, you will be back in the matrix, feeling lost in the chaos of existence. When this happens I need you to come to this last step and remember who you are through the enlightenment that comes from going inside. There is a saying, "A mountain before enlightenment is a mountain, a mountain during enlightenment is no longer a mountain, and a mountain after enlightenment is a mountain again." It's crucial that you take at least <u>20 minutes a day</u> to remember what you learned about your own mountain.

Step 1 – Quiet the Voices: There is no exact science to meditate. Don't concern yourself with the proper way to sit, the placement of your legs, specific Yoga breathing, or the time of day. Feel free to develop your own technique without being a slave to any one form. Pick a quiet place. Sit comfortably. Turn off anything that could distract you like a phone or TV. Close your eyes. Try to turn your thoughts off... not easy, right? Your first thought will be, "think about not thinking," but that's a Catch-22. Instead of trying to end thoughts, focus them on something. Your own breathing. A number. An image. The memory of a sound that was soothing. Let that anchor you until you forget that you were supposed to be thinking about it in the first place. Don't focus on what you have to do later on or a person you need to check in with and don't try to use this meditation as a chance to make wishes for the universe to grant. No goal orientated thought should be in your mind, quiet all voices.

Step 2 – Question: You know who you are but go back to who you were. The lingering emotions that you have yet to overcome from the past should be the first level of going inside. Every session you should revisit the past you. This is a deeper therapy than you can do with another person. Confront the things you still hate, regret, and fear instead of running from them. The parent that didn't raise you properly, the boy that broke your heart, the death of someone you loved. Whatever your character's lingering issues are, go there. Feel the sadness all over again. Do you blame them? Do you blame yourself? Do you want to blame it on Karma or the old religious view that it was punishment for something? Question all your old beliefs about "Why" bad things and good things happen.

Question the concept of good and evil itself. Question right and wrong. Question your morals. Question things you hate and love. Question the thoughts that turn you on and off sexually. All of the taboo things you run from, stand still and confront them. You have been operating a character based on guilt and shame. Let go of that bullshit. If this world and everything in it is you, then how can you hate anything? If all roads lead to your evolution, then how can anything be evil? If something makes you feel good without being at the expense of someone else, how can that be wrong? Who has made the rules that you used to follow? Other people. You are no longer a slave to anyone's "word" you are a Master. Push guilt from your mind at this point. Detach yourself from that character and look from above at your old life like a bird looks down at sheep in a field. Are you that person who went through that pain or are you evolved beyond that struggle? Are you going to always make excuses, always make assumptions, and always be down on yourself based on the past, or can you now with your eyes closed in the dark, accept that it's time to let go of those human emotions that keep you in a limiting mindset? Who are you? Tell yourself.

Step 3 – Reveal: You are not the body you are in. Your mind is not the physical brain in your head. You are not the name that your parents gave you. You are not the way your friends think of you, the degree you have, or the job you hold. The real you, that's who I want you to connect with. The voice in your head at this moment of deep meditation. Listen to it. Ask it questions. Have a conversation. Embrace that voice and understand who you really are. Breathe and push out all of the superstition. Breathe and push out all the beliefs. Breathe and push out all of the brainwashing that you have done to yourself by listening to everyone except your own inner voice. Kill the old concept you once called "self". The drama of your story, the noise of other people, the insignificant buzzing of the so-called "real world," none of that will matter at the moment of total calmness and self-reflection. Hold on to that for as long as you can.

When you wake up the mountain will once again be a mountain, but meditation will always be there to give you a reminder that will put everything back into perspective. There is no stress, no unfairness, no pressure to do anything or to be anyone, only the truth of your existence. No matter if it's the morning, the afternoon, or the evening, go inside and remember who you are. This is the third step, but from this day forward, you have to repeat it for at least 20 minutes a day. Get to know yourself and the path will remain lit.

Illuminate

Why would you cry over a boy, a job, missed opportunities, money, or any other thing life throws at you? *In the end you win.* Remember those words. Your universe is created with you at the center. The Human Game started you off with limits for a reason. Are you going to complain or follow the clues that will allow you to overcome those limits? The meaning of your life is right there, nothing is hidden! Your life isn't about amassing points to get into some heaven, reincarnation, or worshipping false idols. It is about your rise to the top. Will you give into the negative and live a life where you are always losing, always settling, always struggling with only pockets of greatness? Or will you give into the positive and accept that you can and will have everything you deserve, not in the end, but in the now?

Know yourself. Your real self, not your story character or the ego-based personality. Open your eyes, keep them open, and stop being caught up in the game as if it's real! Stop hypnotizing yourself to be like the rest of them. No more listening to advice from the unenlightened. No more wanting to fit in and be normal. No more external projections influencing your internal core. Watch your words and understand your actions. Don't say things like "luck" "hope" "wish" or point fingers at "they" as if your life is a game of chance being dictated by other people or groups. A victim mindset is one where the blame is laid at the feet of oppressors. A Goddess mindset is one where you know there is nothing that can stop you because it is all you! If you live your life like a Spartan, guided by Goddess Consciousness without the noise of doubt, life will change instantaneously. Overthinking, worrying, being moody, none of those things will affect you the higher you rise. The chains of life are all imaginary. Your true nature is the highest power ever created. Live by that nature, cast off those chains, and be reborn! Understand who you are, understand what you want, and understand that it is already yours!

*Continued in, **Men Don't Love Women Like You**...*
Section II - Date Like a Spartan

If you loved these bonus chapters, read the full books:

Solving Single

She Ain't It

Men Don't Love Women Like You

Ho Tactics: The Savage Edition

Deluxe Editions Available @ SolvingSingle.com

Made in the USA
San Bernardino, CA
26 November 2018